The Cambridge Introduction to
Walter Benjamin

For students of modern criticism and theory, Walter Benjamin's
writings have become essential reading. His analyses of photography,
film, language, material culture, and the poet Charles Baudelaire, and
his vast examination of the social, political, and historical significance of
the Arcades of nineteenth-century Paris have left an enduring and
important critical legacy. This volume examines in detail a substantial
selection of his important critical writings on these topics from 1916 to
1940 and outlines his life in pre-war Germany, his association with the
Frankfurt School, and the dissemination of his ideas and methodologies
into a variety of academic disciplines since his death. David Ferris traces
the development of Benjamin's key critical concepts and provides
students with an accessible overview of the life, work, and thought of one
of the twentieth century's most important literary and cultural critics.

David S. Ferris is Professor of Comparative Literature at the University
of Colorado at Boulder.

T0364208

The Cambridge Introduction to
Walter Benjamin

DAVID S. FERRIS

CAMBRIDGE
UNIVERSITY PRESS

CAMBRIDGE UNIVERSITY PRESS
Cambridge, New York, Melbourne, Madrid, Cape Town,
Singapore, São Paulo, Delhi, Tokyo, Mexico City

Cambridge University Press
The Edinburgh Building, Cambridge CB2 8RU, UK

Published in the United States of America by Cambridge University Press, New York

www.cambridge.org
Information on this title: www.cambridge.org/9780521683081

First published 2008

A catalogue record for this publication is available from the British Library

Library of Congress Cataloging-in-Publication Data
Ferris, David S., 1954–
The Cambridge introduction to Walter Benjamin / David S. Ferris.
   p.   cm.
Includes bibliographical references and index.
ISBN 978-0-521-86458-9
1. Benjamin, Walter, 1892–1940 – Criticism and interpretation. I. Title.
PT2603.E455Z648   2008
838'.91209 – dc22   2008029277

ISBN 978-0-521-86458-9 Hardback
ISBN 978-0-521-68308-1 Paperback

"Images – my great, my primitive passion."
Walter Benjamin

Contents

Preface

To present the work of Walter Benjamin in the form of an introduction requires a willingness to face the challenge posed by a body of work recognized for its range and the difficulty of its concepts, as well as this critic's recursive and frequently elliptical writing style. But these are not the only reasons that an introduction to Benjamin is challenging. Another, potentially more important reason is given by Benjamin in a note he writes for himself in 1930–31:

> Examine the sense in which "Outlines," "Guides" and so on are touchstones for the state of a discipline. Show that they are the most demanding of all, and how clearly their phrasing betrays every half-measure.

In many respects, any introduction to Benjamin will now be a reflection of the state of the discipline since his work has found its way into so many corners of the humanities and social sciences. At the same time, an introduction makes demands that the professionalization of critical writing happily ignores. These demands increase greatly when the subject is Walter Benjamin. Faced with a critic who had the clear-sightedness to see his own work as "a contradictory and mobile whole," the task of grasping the nature of that whole, its contradictions, its mobility, almost ensures that every phrase betrays a measure not yet achieved. Yet, there is some justice – of a Benjaminian kind – in such a betrayal. If an introduction has a story to tell, it should be such a story. Only then can its most important task be fulfilled: to point beyond itself while laying the paths that lead towards the challenges posed by Benjamin's work.

Today, foremost among these challenges is the sheer amount of material that has been made available by the collected editions of his writings and letters published in Germany. Recently, the publication in English of Benjamin's *Selected Writings* has provided access to the many additional texts, fragments, and notes that were only available in German. Despite the amount of this material, many of the works available before the appearance of the *Selected Writings* still claim the attention of an introduction since it is with these works that many students have their first experience of Benjamin. Accordingly, most of the works that make up the canon of Benjamin's *œuvre* are presented here. Within these works, emphasis has been placed on the writings that allow a sense of Benjamin's critical development to appear. Because of the desire to keep this series of introductions to a reasonable length, it was, unfortunately, not possible to present some works that might otherwise have been included, such as, for example, the essays "Unpacking My Library," "Eduard Fuchs, Collector and Historian," and "Problems in the Sociology of Language." Other works are mentioned only in passing whenever they have direct relevance to another topic or concept. Throughout, the organizing principle has emphasized those works that map the ways in which Benjamin's thinking evolves from the metaphysical tendencies of his university years through to the dialectical and materialist analyses of his last years. Almost everywhere, the mobility of this evolution is tempered by the contradictions it produced – contradictions that propelled much of Benjamin's best work even if many of them were to remain unresolved if not unresolvable.

Acknowledgments

Special thanks are due to Graham Oddie, Associate Dean of Arts and Sciences at the University of Colorado, Boulder – his support helped the writing of this introduction at a crucial stage; to Hannah Blanning and Tonja van Helden who served as research assistants in spring and fall 2007; to Patricia Paige who zealously protected my time with her superlative administrative skills and tact; to the students who participated in my seminars on Benjamin in New York and Colorado; and to colleagues whose writing on Benjamin has informed, questioned and, at times, ran parallel to my own: Andrew Benjamin, Eduardo Cadava, Howard Caygill, Rebecca Comay, Peter Fenves, Rodolphe Gasché, Werner Hamacher, Carol Jacobs, Michael Jennings, Rainer Nägele, Henry Sussman, and Samuel Weber.

List of abbreviations

The following abbreviations and short titles refer to works listed below. In each case, the abbreviation will be followed by a page number (e.g. *C*, 21), or in the case of the German edition of Benjamin's writings, by volume, part, and page number (e.g., *GS* 7.2, 532). On occasion, some of the translations used in this volume have been modified from the published versions. Full bibliographical information for the volumes listed below is included in the Guide to Further Reading.

AB	*Adorno and Benjamin: The Complete Correspondence 1928–1940*
AP	*The Arcades Project*
C	*The Correspondence of Walter Benjamin 1920–1940*
Chronicle	*A Berlin Chronicle*
Friendship	*Walter Benjamin: The Story of a Friendship*
GB	*Gesammelte Briefe*
GS	*Gesammelte Schriften*
OGT	*Origin of the German Tragic Drama*
SW	*Selected Writings 1913–1940*

Life

A life displaced

An account of Benjamin's life is in many ways an account of the financial and intellectual obstacles Benjamin faced during the twenty years he became the foremost cultural critic of his generation. It is also an account of someone who traveled widely through Europe, from Capri to Spain to Moscow to the Arctic Circle and, above all, to the one place that kept such a hold on his critical imagination, Paris; it is an account of the person who came to know and correspond with most of the leading intellectuals and writers of his time – Rainer Maria Rilke, André Gide, Hugo von Hofmannstahl, Georges Bataille, Theodor Adorno, Max Horkheimer, Ernst Robert Curtius, Florens Christian Rang, Ernst Bloch, Bertolt Brecht, Gershom Scholem, Hannah Arendt, Paul Valéry, Hermann Hesse, André Malraux, the photographer Germaine Krull, among many others; of the person who translated Proust and Baudelaire; of the person who used a series of pseudonyms for publishing out of personal choice and political necessity – Ardor, C. Conrad, K. A. Stempflinger, Detlev Holz, Hans Fellner, J. E. Mabinn (an anagram of Benjamin), and O. E. Tal (an anagram of *lateo*: I am concealed); of the person who wrote for newspapers and journals, performed radio broadcasts; of the person whose writing spanned the autobiographical, the critical, the academic thesis, poetry, the short story, and radio plays for children; and finally of the person who collected toys and children's books in addition to his own extensive literary and philosophical library.

As this list indicates, Benjamin's life is the intellectual life of a generation and its cultural and historical contexts. The merely personal pales in comparison. Perhaps, we should expect no less from someone who famously declared his avoidance of the word "I" except in letters. For this reason, a biography of Benjamin is dominated by the history of his intellectual engagements and their intersection with the geographical displacements that defined his life as well as his friendships.

1892–1912 Berlin: childhood and school years

> My thinking always has Wyneken, my first teacher, as its starting point and always returns to him.

Walter Benjamin is born in Berlin on July 15, 1892, the first of Emil and Pauline Benjamin's three children – his brother Georg is born in 1895 and his sister Dora in 1901. His early years provide the privileges of an upper-middle-class childhood (a governess, schooled at home) at a time when Berlin is emerging as one of Europe's principal metropolitan centers. During his childhood, the family moves several times but remains within the upper-middle-class neighborhoods that arose to the west of central Berlin. Benjamin's childhood excursions out of these neighborhoods are always under the wing of his mother or governess with the result that he lacks the freedom to explore the city without constraint or oversight – a situation he draws attention to in his *Berlin Chronicle* when he looks back at these years as a time when he was "enclosed" in "the old and new West End" (*Chronicle*, SW 2, 599–600).

Benjamin's first move out of this sheltered situation occurs when, just before his ninth birthday, he is enrolled in one of Berlin's better secondary schools, the Kaiser Friedrich School. Prior to this Benjamin has only received private tutoring. His recollections of the Kaiser Friedrich School are not fond. When Benjamin recalls its classrooms, he writes that "little … has remained in my memory except those perfect emblems of imprisonment: the frosted windows and infamous carved wooden embattlements over the doors" (*Chronicle*, SW 2, 602). Indeed, the little he does remember takes the form of "catastrophic encounters." In addition, his time there is punctuated by illnesses resulting in the 1904 decision by his parents to withdraw him from the school.

In 1905, after several months without formal instruction, Benjamin is sent to a country boarding school in the town of Haubinda, several hundred miles southwest of Berlin. His parents see this country setting as an opportunity to improve his health. For Benjamin, it came to offer a far different opportunity.

The school in Haubinda was a progressive counter-cultural institution founded in 1901. While there he comes into contact with an educational reformer, Gustav Wyneken, who was on the teaching staff at that time. Wyneken's ideas on youth culture and the reform of youth education subsequently exert considerable influence on the young Benjamin. Wyneken advocated a curriculum based on what he called the solidarity of youth, an aspect Wyneken found in the drive towards spiritual and intellectual independence that youth naturally possessed. For Wyneken, development of this tendency is part of a larger project that aims at a cultural revolution of society through its youth. While the influence of Wyneken's educational theories is present in the essays Benjamin writes between 1910 and 1915, the major, immediate effect of Benjamin's time at Haubinda is the development of his interest in German literature and philosophy.

In 1907 Benjamin returns to Berlin and again enrolls at the Kaiser Friedrich School. Despite the obvious pressure to conform to the traditional curriculum and manner of instruction at Kaiser Friedrich, Benjamin retains what he learned at Haubinda:

> Since my return from Haubinda my philosophical and literary interests developed generally into a specifically aesthetic interest, a natural synthesis. I pursued this through an engagement partly with the theory of drama and partly with great plays, most notably those of Shakespeare, Hebbel and Ibsen; alongside the close study of Hamlet and Tasso I also pursued a thorough engagement with Hölderlin. Above all, these interests expressed themselves in the attempt to form my own judgment on literary issues.[1]

In addition to this study of literature, Benjamin now turns to philosophy "in order to obtain an overview of its problems and the systems of its great thinkers."[2] At the same time, he starts to address a major shortcoming of the classical curriculum at the Kaiser Friedrich School: its exclusion of any serious study of modern literature. As Benjamin recalls in 1913, the most modern writer taught was Kleist (1777–1811) but, perhaps more devastating for Benjamin, this teaching "did not concern itself with a serious relation to works of art."[3] As a result, Benjamin and a small group of friends form a weekly literary evening to discuss works and writers ignored by the school curriculum.

Benjamin's first published writings date from the last years of his secondary schooling. Several poems and some essays appear under the pseudonym "Ardor" in a school magazine entitled *Der Anfang* (The Beginning). The use of a pseudonym is apparently meant to shield Benjamin from reprisals by the school authorities on account of what he has written. At the same time, the association of the word ardor with fervor, passion, and zeal points to those qualities of youth that Benjamin has learned to value under Wyneken's instruction at Haubinda. While these early writings can be seen as embodying such qualities, subsequent writings for this magazine (published during his early university years) show a willingness to advocate for Wyneken's educational reforms as well as theorize about education itself.

1912–1917 University, war, and marriage

> The only thing you get out of [Cohn's seminar on the *Critique of Judgment* and Schiller's aesthetics] is that you read the texts.

After completing his final examinations at the Kaiser Friedrich School in March 1912 and after a short trip to Italy, Benjamin enrolls at the Albert Ludwigs University in Freiburg im Breisgau in order to study philosophy. This first semester leaves much to be desired from an intellectual standpoint. Compared to his school years, and in particular to the weekly discussion meetings among his friends, Freiburg offers him little. In a letter from June of this year, Benjamin summarizes his expectations and experience at Freiburg: "it is impossible to harvest while one is plowing" (*C*, 16). Benjamin's studies at Freiburg clearly lack the engagement with the problems and issues posed by modern experience that have so attracted him during his school years. As a result, he not only takes up the question of school reform advocated by Wyneken but also decides to return to Berlin for the second semester of his university studies.

In October 1912, Benjamin enrolls at the Royal Wilhelm Friedrich University in Berlin. During his first semester there, he attends lectures by Ernst Cassirer, a neo-Kantian best known for his philosophy of symbolic forms, Benno Erdmann, also a Kantian philosopher, Adolph Goldschmidt, the German art critic and historian, Max Erdman, a leading Kantian scholar, and the social and economics philosopher Georg Simmel. He becomes more involved in the school reform movement and renews his contact with Wyneken even to the point of declaring himself his "strict and fanatical disciple" (*GB* 1, 64). He also secures election as president of the Free Students Association. Despite this commitment to the student movement in Berlin, Benjamin fails to win re-election as president in the spring of 1913 and, as a result, decides to return to Freiburg for the summer semester.

During his second semester in Freiburg, Benjamin attends lectures given by the neo-Kantian philosopher Heinrich Rickert, as does Martin Heidegger. Rickert's lectures do not captivate the young Benjamin, who reports: "I . . . just sit and pursue my own thoughts in Rickert's seminar. After the seminar, Keller and I go to the Marienbad, agree with each other, and believe ourselves to be more incisive than Rickert" (*C*, 31). Benjamin continues his commitment to school reform while in Freiburg. He hopes it will have a greater reception in the setting where Wyneken's ideas were first received by university students. Instead, what he experiences are tensions about both the direction the movement should take and its involvement in politics and culture. These tensions surface prominently around the magazine *Der Anfang* – the same magazine of his school days which now appears in a regular edition from an established publisher. Benjamin's position is that *Der Anfang* "absolutely must remain a purely intellectual (not aesthetic or some such) publication, yet removed from politics." The difficulty of holding to this position becomes even clearer to Benjamin after his return to Berlin in September 1913.

The tensions surrounding *Der Anfang* reflect strategic differences within the school reform movement (as well as the pull of the different groups advocating reform). These differences emphasize Benjamin's tendency to seek a purer, more philosophical understanding. In a letter from 1913, he expresses this as "a purity of spirit" but, at the same time, recognizes that such an understanding runs the risk of being restricted by its own goals:

> To be young does not mean so much serving the spirit as awaiting it ...
> the concept of youth culture should simply be illumination that draws
> even the most remote spirit to its light. For many people, however,
> Wyneken ... will be merely a "movement." They will have committed
> themselves and will no longer see the spirit where it manifests itself as
> freer and more abstract. This constantly reverberating feeling for the
> abstractness of pure spirit I would like to call youth. (*C*, 54–55)

The purity of idea and spirit Benjamin expresses here provides an important index to his intellectual development at this time. What Benjamin sees in Wyneken is the idea of youth as something to be preserved. Even when Benjamin breaks with Wyneken in 1915 after Wyneken expresses support for German participation in the First World War, his separation takes the form of trying to preserve this purity of idea even though, as he later recognizes, it was bound to fail (*Chronicle*, *SW* 2, 605).

Benjamin confronts other movements at this time, most notably Zionism. His encounter with this movement occurs in August 1912 when another student attempts to convert him to political Zionism while he is on vacation in Poland. Although Benjamin will eventually reject a politically based Zionism, during the next two years he does engage in a correspondence with Ludwig Strauß, a student Benjamin knew from Freiburg, about the significance and purpose of

Zionism as well as his relation to it. In one of these letters, from October 1912, Benjamin strongly critiques Zionists and distinguishes their position from the experience of being Jewish:

> Their [the Zionists] personality was not inwardly determined in any way by Jewishness: they propagate Palestine but drink like Germans. Perhaps these people are necessary but they are the last people who should talk of the Jewish experience. They are brutes (*Halbmenschen*). Have they ever reflected upon schools, literature, the inner life, and the state in a Jewish way? (*GB* 1, 72)

While Benjamin strongly rejects Zionism with these words, it is also clear that he attaches considerable significance to the experience of being Jewish – even to the point of associating such an experience with the questions that attracted him the most during his formative school and university years. Indeed, in the same letter, he observes that there is something in Wyneken's ideas that permits "a close inward influence on himself and other Jews" (*GB* 1, 71). Here, as in the break with Wyneken in 1915, Benjamin preserves what has become significant for him. He rejects movements that seek simpler, concrete resolutions to the kinds of issues he will treat with greater historical complexity in the years ahead.

In late spring of 1914, Benjamin's letters begin to mention a love interest in Grete Radt, the sister of Fritz Radt, a fellow student in Berlin. Benjamin speaks fondly of her as the "only person who sees and comprehends me in my totality" (*C*, 66). In July, after returning to Berlin, he announces his engagement to Grete. Alongside this development in his personal life, 1914 also marks Benjamin's first experience with personal loss. At Freiburg, he has developed a close friendship with another student, Fritz Heinle, whose poetry he champions and seeks to have published in the journal *Der Anfang*. In 1914, Heinle and another student who has been active in the youth movement, Rika Seligson, commit suicide four days after the German invasion of Belgium. Their suicide takes place in the room that Benjamin and his friends in the youth movement have been using for their meetings. The choice of location underlines the ideals of youth and the denial of these ideals by the advent of war. With Heinle's and Seligson's death the enthusiasm he and his friends expressed when they initially sought to enlist together to fight in the war evaporates. This double suicide leads to a period of depression for Benjamin. He finds little to interest him as he resumes his university studies in Berlin. At the next call-up of his age group, Benjamin fakes suffering from palsy in order to avoid conscription. He is successful and receives a year's deferment.

In 1915, Benjamin begins a friendship with Gershom Scholem that will continue for the rest of his life – one of the few relationships he sustains for such a period of time even though it will have its difficult moments in the 1930s. With Scholem, Benjamin again experiences the pull of Zionism and his Jewish identity, topics on which they frequently converse. At the same time, his attachment to Grete Radt remains strong. In the fall of 1915, he follows her to Munich where she is enrolled at the Ludwig-Maximilian University. Benjamin also enrolls there but, beyond his love interest in Grete, Munich provides little stimulation. The university, he reports, is worse than Berlin – and Benjamin does not have a high opinion of Berlin. Although Benjamin continues to contemplate an academic career well into the 1920s, the conflicted relation he will display towards academic study is already present in these years, most notably in his repeated characterization of the university as a place of intellectual failure rather than achievement – a letter from this time even indicts the contemporary university as "a swamp" (*C*, 74).

By early 1916, Benjamin's engagement to Grete gives way to his developing relationship with Dora Pollack who has separated from her husband Max. Prior to the war, Benjamin has known both Max and Dora through the youth movement in Berlin. This will be one of several amorous relationships Benjamin eventually pursues amongst his circle of friends. While his interest in Dora develops he also begins to receive intellectual recognition. In June, Martin Buber invites him to contribute to his journal, *Der Jude*, but Benjamin declines on the grounds that the theory of language he is then developing precludes the kind of link between writing and politics that Buber advocates through this journal. The theory of language Benjamin refers to here is the subject of the essay "On Language as Such and on the Languages of Man" he completes this same year. In this refusal to contribute, there reappears a characteristic Benjamin has already displayed in his break with Wyneken: an uncompromising commitment to a purity of thinking that resists predetermined expectations.

In late 1916, Benjamin is again subject to a draft review after having already received two deferments (he had obtained a second deferment in 1915 after drinking an excessive amount of coffee the night before his fitness for duty is to be evaluated). This time he is declared fit for duty but manages to avoid service after suffering an attack of sciatica. Having avoided the draft, Benjamin remains enrolled as a student in Munich but he excuses himself from all courses in November 1916 and only registers for one course during the summer semester of 1917 – ostensibly in order to retain library privileges. During this time, he continues to work on his translations of Baudelaire and begins the study of a nineteenth-century work on the Kabbalah he has received from Scholem. The projects Benjamin pursues this year involve topics that he will return to through much of his subsequent career. As such, 1917 marks the beginning of the more strongly philosophical, literary, and critical direction that characterizes his best-known early publications. The year 1917 also marks a new beginning in his personal life; in April, he and Dora are married.

1917–1925 Pursuit of an academic career

> In many periods, there has been sterile scholarship, certainly more sterile than in our own time, the shamelessness of scholarly study is however modern.

In the fall of 1917, Benjamin enrolls at the University of Berne in order to undertake a doctoral dissertation. This decision also has a welcome consequence: by studying in Switzerland, Benjamin will no longer have to worry about being drafted for military service. The subject Benjamin pursues for his dissertation is the philosophical basis of the theory of criticism developed within German Romanticism, most notably in the work of Friedrich Schlegel and Novalis. The intertwining of philosophical and literary interests that will characterize much of his academic writing in the coming years is strongly present in this project, as is an abiding interest in the formation of the modern concept of criticism. Benjamin's first semester of doctoral study is also marked by the writing of "On the Program of the Coming Philosophy," an unpublished essay in which Benjamin proclaims the need to preserve what is essential in Kant's thought while undertaking the attempt to attain an "epistemological foundation for a higher concept of experience" (*SW* 1, 102). The struggle between academic life and his own interests resurfaces in Berne. Benjamin is forced to wonder if his work on the dissertation "is not wasted time" (*C*, 136). Despite this concern, he produces a draft of the dissertation by April 1919 and then defends it in June. Benjamin judges the dissertation to be "a pointer to the true nature of romanticism" that does not, however, "get to the heart of romanticism" (*C*, 139–40). The reason for this failing is the need to provide "the expected complicated and conventional scholarly attitude," an attitude he distinguishes from a "genuine" scholarly attitude. This sense of a mismatch between his interests and formal academic expectations is now mixed in with the precarious financial situation in which he and Dora find themselves as well as the new responsibility of caring for Stefan Rafael, their only child, born in April 1918. Despite the willingness of his doctoral dissertation advisor to supervise further research, their financial situation, compounded by rising inflation, puts an end to any possibility of pursuing his academic studies in Berne.

To eventually secure an academic position, Benjamin will have to write a second dissertation in order to receive what is called the Habilitation – without the Habilitation it is impossible to obtain a teaching position in the German university system. The Habilitation also requires the support of a university advisor, a condition that proves to be the greatest obstacle Benjamin faces. By March 1920, Benjamin has still not secured the requisite support. Compounding this problem, their financial situation has worsened to such an extent that they have no choice but to move in with Benjamin's parents in Berlin. However, tensions between Benjamin and his parents soon compel them to move out. They manage to support themselves until September but are then forced to move back in again with Benjamin's parents.

Despite these financial troubles, Benjamin still pursues his plan to obtain the Habilitation. He also embarks on other literary and critical projects, notably his long essay on Goethe's novel, *The Elective Affinities*. As many commentators have pointed out, there is considerable irony to be attached to Benjamin's work on Goethe's novel at this time since Benjamin's personal life begins to resemble the tangled relationships of Goethe's characters. Early in 1921, Benjamin's marriage unravels. Dora falls in love with one of their friends, Ernst Schoen. In April, Benjamin falls in love with Jula Cohn, the sister of a friend from his days at the Kaiser Friedrich School. Scholem recalls that both "were convinced that they had now experienced the love of their lives" (*Friendship*, 115–16). During the summer, Benjamin continues his relationship with Jula in Heidelberg. While there, he attempts to gain acceptance as a student for the Habilitation but despite his confidence that he has done everything necessary, he is refused in November 1922. During the two months he spends in Heidelberg, Benjamin also attends lectures by the literary critic Friedrich Gundolf, one of the main figures in the literary circle surrounding the poet Stefan George. Despite Gundolf's literary and critical reputation (Gundolf's 1916 book on Goethe has been regarded as an important rediscovery of Goethe), Benjamin is not impressed. Benjamin later makes Gundolf's critical approach, and with it the approach of the George School, the target of an uncompromising critique in his essay on Goethe's *Elective Affinities*. Benjamin's harshness is an attempt to bring down the reigning critical orthodoxy in Germany at this time while establishing his own voice and a different mode of critical interpretation. However, when the essay is finally published in 1928, it receives little attention.

In 1921, Benjamin announces a new project: the launch of a journal to be named after a drawing by Paul Klee which Benjamin had bought in the spring of that year, the "Angelus Novus" – a drawing Benjamin will keep with him through his remaining years in Germany and subsequent exile. Benjamin's stated aim in this journal is to "restore criticism to its former strength" by recognizing its foremost task, namely, to "account for the truth of works," a task he considers "just as essential for literature as for philosophy" (*SW* 1,

293). The primacy Benjamin gives to this task recognizes the centrality of criticism as the means by which the modern age makes its claim to historical significance.

As Benjamin attempts to bring this project to fruition during 1922, he strikes up a friendship with the conservative Christian intellectual Florens Christian Rang, whom he had first met in Berlin in 1918. This friendship is one of the incongruities Benjamin often displays. Scholem explains it as an attraction of opposites (*Friendship*, 116), yet Benjamin's reverence for Rang goes beyond this cliché. In a 1923 letter, Benjamin proclaims, in all sincerity, that Rang represents "genuine Germanness" (*C*, 214), a remark that shows how strong Benjamin's ties to a German identity are at this time. For Benjamin, this identity cannot be divorced from what is essential to his critical and intellectual interests. More practically, Rang is instrumental in introducing Benjamin to Hugo von Hofmannsthal, the leading literary figure of this time. Hofmannsthal quickly recognizes Benjamin's significance and helps secure the publication of his essay on Goethe's *Elective Affinities*.

In late 1922, Benjamin renews his efforts to obtain the Habilitation, spurred on by an ultimatum from his father that "any further support would be contingent on [Benjamin] taking a job in a bank" (*C*, 201). In December, he goes to Frankfurt to explore possibilities there but finds little encouragement. The difficulty of Benjamin's situation weighs on him and, at the beginning of 1923, he suffers from depression. Despite his slim prospects at Frankfurt, he remains determined to write the second dissertation in the belief that it would be "better to be chased off in disgrace than to retreat" (*C*, 209).

Finding a university and a faculty willing to take on his project – a study of little-read plays from the Baroque period – is just one of the many problems Benjamin experiences in 1923. His living conditions have not improved and Jula turns out not to be the love of his life. In spite of their affairs, Dora and Benjamin remain friends and, out of financial need, continue a shared living arrangement (although this will change by November). Their situation affects them heavily. Benjamin speaks of "the misery into which we are increasingly dragged" (*C*, 209). Dora becomes ill. In addition, external conditions are bleak: the Weimar Republic has collapsed, inflation is rampant, and above all else there is the "paralyzing effect" of the "decline of the university" (*C*, 209). With so much falling apart, Benjamin contemplates following his friend Scholem to Palestine but, barely two months later, declares that Palestine is "neither a practical nor a theoretical possibility" (*C*, 216). In spite of all this hardship, 1923 marks one of the most significant years in Benjamin's intellectual journey. He experiments with a different kind of writing, one no longer defined by academic literary and critical demands. This writing will produce the volume entitled

One-Way Street, a series of "thought-images" that announce Benjamin's turn towards a more politically informed cultural criticism.

The direction Benjamin takes in *One-Way Street* receives a strong push in 1924 from Asja Lacis, a Bolshevik theater director and performer from Latvia whom Benjamin meets during a six-month stay on the island of Capri. While Capri affords him the time to continue work on his Habilitation thesis, Lacis also exposes him directly to radical left-wing politics. As a result of this exposure, Benjamin reads the work of the Hungarian Marxist critic Georg Lukács, specifically his seminal book *History and Class Consciousness*. At this time, Benjamin also turns his attention, for the first time, to Marx's writings. Once back in Berlin at the end of 1924, Benjamin summarizes this turn in a letter to his friend Scholem:

> I hope some day the Communist signals will come through to you more clearly than they did from Capri. At first, they were indications of a change that awakened in me the will not to mask certain actual and political elements of my ideas in the old Franconian way I did before, but also to develop them by experimenting and taking extreme measures. This of course means that the literary exegesis of German literature will now take a back seat.   (*C*, 257–58)

This last sentence signals the most significant turning point in Benjamin's career. It comes at a moment when Benjamin is poised to complete his thesis on Baroque drama. In this case, it is not surprising that Benjamin writes early in 1925 that the thesis project "marks an end for me." Even after securing the support of an advisor at the University of Frankfurt, Franz Schulz, the prospect of an academic position has little appeal. Benjamin is emphatic: "I dread almost everything that would result from a positive resolution to all of this: I dread Frankfurt above all, then lectures, students, etc. Things that take a murderous toll on time" (*C*, 261). This antipathy is confirmed by the reception his thesis receives when he formally submits it in May. Schulz withdraws his support and recommends that Benjamin submit it to Hans Cornelius, a professor in aesthetics, rather than in his field, literary history. Cornelius declares that he is unable to understand it and passes the thesis to two colleagues who have the same response (one of these two colleagues is Max Horkheimer who, with Adorno, is a founding figure of the Frankfurt School and later becomes, in the 1930s, a friend and correspondent of Benjamin). In August, Benjamin withdraws his thesis from further consideration. Thus ends Benjamin's protracted and uncomfortable relation with academic criticism and the university.

The end of this chapter in Benjamin's career is accompanied by an improvement in his financial situation as a result of his publishing activity in late 1924 and 1925; he receives a publishing contract for the rejected thesis, the Goethe essay, and *One-Way Street*, his work in progress. He also secures a position as a regular contributor to the *Frankfurter Zeitung*, a newspaper with a strong democratic and intellectual reputation at the time, and he becomes one of the principal contributors to a new literary journal, *Die Literarische Welt*. As a result of this improvement in his situation, Benjamin can afford to set off from Berlin in August for several months of traveling through Italy and Spain and then finally to Riga where Asja Lacis's theater is based. The hope of pursuing an amorous relationship with Asja comes to nothing and, at the end of December, he returns to Berlin.

1925–1933 Critical ambitions

> I will generate a "politics" from within myself.

Benjamin's increased publishing activity in 1925 indicates how much he has established a critical reputation for himself. Despite this success Asja's refusal to continue their affair during his trip to Riga in late 1925 leaves him despondent and unproductive. In response, he throws himself into reading what he describes as "a sinful quantity of things," an activity that distracts him from completing *One-Way Street* and from making progress on a commission to translate Proust's *A la recherche du temps perdu*. Only later, in 1926, while in Paris, does Benjamin concentrate on the Proust translation. July also brings news of his father's death. Then, in November, after returning to Berlin, he receives word of Asja Lacis's nervous breakdown and rushes to Moscow. Benjamin stays in Moscow from the beginning of December until the beginning of February 1927 but, as before, Lacis has a different view of their affair. An entry from his *Moscow Diary* captures the actual state of this relationship:

> to live in Europe with her – this could one day become the most important, the most tangible thing for me, if only she could be won over to it. In Russia – I have my doubts. We took a sleigh back to the apartment, hugged closely together. It was dark. This was the only moment in the dark that we had shared in Moscow – out in the middle of the street, on the narrow seat of a sleigh.   (*Moscow Diary*, 109)

His stay in Moscow leads him to reflect on the choice prompted by his new political leanings: joining the Communist Party or maintaining his independence as a "left-wing outsider" (*Moscow Diary*, 72). Benjamin decides "to avoid the extremes of 'materialism'" giving the excuse, "as long as I continue to travel, joining the party is obviously something fairly inconceivable" (*Moscow Diary*, 73). Benjamin will remain a traveler through the different intellectual and political forces he explored in these years. In doing so, he preserves his political independence but does so through a recurrent pattern: his tendency to pull back wherever external institutions and organizations impose themselves.

Benjamin does not stay long in Berlin after his return from Moscow but sets out again for Paris in April 1927. He remains married to Dora but it is a marriage based more on friendship than on amorous commitment. Dora, with their son Stefan, visits Benjamin in Paris; they travel to the south of France and, after Benjamin wins some money gambling at the casino in Monte Carlo, they go on vacation together in Corsica. Their relationship remains one that neither of them appears willing to break. But this will change in 1929 when Benjamin requests a divorce, a move that shocks and angers Dora, particularly since Benjamin's legal reason for this request accuses her of infidelity. The depth of Dora's indignation can be gauged from her demand in August 1929 that Benjamin move out of his parents' house (where they have been living with his mother). While infidelity is the legal claim for Benjamin for divorce, the real reason is that Asja Lacis has returned to Berlin. During an earlier visit at the end of 1928 they had resumed their relationship. Benjamin envisages marrying Lacis so that he can give her German citizenship. Hence, the sudden desire to divorce Dora. The divorce worsens Benjamin's financial situation. In the divorce proceedings, he is judged to be the party at fault in the failure of marriage and, as settlement, he is ordered to pay Dora 40,000 marks to compensate her for all the years through which he has largely lived off her income. In order to pay this amount, he is obliged to sign over his inheritance and to part with valuable possessions such as the extensive collection of children's books he has acquired during the 1920s. Despite the divorce, Benjamin and Lacis never marry.

The difficulty of these times again leads Benjamin to consider moving to Palestine. As a favor to his friend, Scholem arranges a meeting in Berlin between Benjamin and the Chancellor of the Hebrew University. The meeting results in Benjamin receiving a stipend to study Hebrew in order to facilitate his eventual emigration to Palestine. When money arrives, Benjamin waits eight months before expressing thanks or even beginning Hebrew lessons. The lessons do not last long. They are discontinued within a month and he does not take them up again. Emigration remains a topic of discussion between Benjamin and Scholem in the 1930s but it is a discussion that quickly settles into a predictable pattern as Benjamin repeatedly equivocates in response to Scholem's requests for a firmer commitment. During this time, it becomes clear to Scholem that the intellectual direction Benjamin is pursuing is quite different from the one that has helped secure support from the Hebrew University. This realization prompts Scholem to remark that Benjamin is "Janus faced" – simultaneously turned towards Communism and Judaism at the same time (*Friendship*, 197, 201).

This period is also marked by Benjamin's increased effort to establish himself as a critic. In January 1930, he writes in a letter to Gershom Scholem:

> I have already carved out a reputation for myself in Germany although of modest proportions ... The goal is that I be considered the foremost critic of German literature. The problem is that literary criticism is no longer considered a serious genre in Germany, and has not been for more than fifty years ... One must thus create criticism as a genre.   (*C*, 359)

Giving a form to this criticism becomes the dominating factor in his work as he assimilates the pull of two important new friendships. The first of these friendships is with Bertolt Brecht, the Marxist playwright and poet best known for his theory of theatrical alienation. The second is with Theodor Adorno, a co-founder of the Institute for Social Research (more commonly known as the Frankfurt School) who practiced a Marxist-influenced brand of social and cultural criticism.

Asja Lacis had introduced Benjamin to Brecht in May 1929. Scholem recalls the influence of Brecht as the arrival of "a new element, an elemental force in the truest sense of the word in [Benjamin's] life" (*Friendship*, 159). Although Benjamin had already experienced an important exposure to Marxism through Asja Lacis and his reading of Lukács, it was not until he formed his friendship with Brecht that this exposure was transformed into a deeper commitment. This transformation resulted from extended conversations in Germany and in Denmark where Benjamin visited Brecht in the summers of 1934, 1936, and 1938.

Brecht's brand of radical political thinking and the influence it exerted is complemented in these years by Benjamin's growing friendship with Adorno. Benjamin's and Adorno's paths had already crossed in the summer of 1923 when both were enrolled in the same seminar in Frankfurt. Early in 1928, they meet in Berlin and begin a friendship that lasted until Benjamin's death. Through Adorno, Benjamin comes into contact with a strong Marxist-oriented current of thought. Yet, Benjamin does not settle easily into the political critique shared by the members of the Frankfurt School, even though its two founders, Adorno and Max Horkheimer, both felt that Benjamin was one of the few who were closest to its critical approach. Benjamin will develop a more idiosyncratic Marxism that incorporates elements of Brecht and the Frankfurt School along with a messianic sense of history.

The early 1930s become increasingly difficult for Benjamin. He is never quite able to overcome his financial difficulties. In addition, there is the changing political climate brought about by the rise of the Nazi movement. In a diary from this time, Benjamin speaks of the hopelessness of any critical position to affect the changing cultural and political situation in Germany. This fatigue, and his own financial situation, not only produces in him a sense "of having lived a life whose dearest wishes had been granted" but also leads him to express a "growing willingness to take my own life" (*SW* 2, 469–70). This contemplation of suicide returns dramatically in August when, under the heading "Diary from August 7, 1931, to the day of my death," he writes: "this diary does not promise to become very long" (*SW* 2, 501). The diary is not very long. After this announcement it veers off into critical observations before being discontinued. The following year, 1932, Benjamin again contemplates suicide – in a hotel in Nice on his fortieth birthday. The possible precipitating cause in this case is the rejection of his offer of marriage by Olga Parem (Benjamin had known her for at least four years and she was also visiting Ibiza while Benjamin was there from April to August). Benjamin does not carry out his intention even though he went so far as to complete a will and compose farewell letters to several friends. A final remark from his 1931 essay "The Destructive Character" could be cited as an explanation: "The destructive character lives from the feeling not that life is worth living, but that suicide is not worth the trouble" (*SW* 2, 542).

The situation in Germany worsens in 1932. The suspension of the Prussian government on July 20 paves the way for the events leading to the installation of Hitler as Chancellor on January 30, 1933. Twenty-eight days after Hitler is sworn in as Chancellor, and less than twenty-four hours after the burning of the Reichstag in Berlin, Benjamin observes: "The little composure that people in my circles were able to muster in the face of the new regime was rapidly spent, and one realizes that the air is hardly fit to breathe anymore – a condition which of course loses significance as one is being strangled anyway. This above all economically."[4] Benjamin's metaphor of strangulation threatens to turn literal as some friends are placed in concentration camps, and others such as Brecht and Siegfried Kracauer go into exile. Another direct consequence of the situation in Germany is the loss of the publishing venues Benjamin had relied on as a source of income. Despite this situation, Benjamin completes and publishes his well-known essay "Little History of Photography" (1931) and, in 1932, completes drafts of his autobiographical text, *Berlin Childhood around 1900*. Still, the financial crisis precipitated by the situation in Germany is such that Benjamin is forced to declare: "I don't know how I will make it through the [coming months], whether inside or outside Germany. There are places where I could earn a minimal income, and places where I could live on a minimal income, but not a single place where these two conditions coincide."[5]

1933–1940 Exile in Paris

> The art of balancing.

In March 1933, Benjamin leaves Berlin definitively. He goes to Paris first and then, in April, travels on to Ibiza where he learns that his brother Georg, who has been an active member of the German Communist Party since the late 1920s, has been arrested (Georg is released in December but is later rearrested and sentenced to six years' imprisonment in 1936). The desperateness of Benjamin's situation once more raises the idea of moving to Palestine. This time, his reluctance is informed by the fear that emigration will mean the abandoning of all that he has accomplished up to this point. Rather than emigrate, Benjamin returns to Paris in October to begin an exile from Germany that will last until his death in 1940.

Benjamin's life in Paris is difficult, intellectually and financially. He complains of loneliness, and by March 1934 he can no longer afford the cheap hotel in which he has been staying since his arrival. At this moment of crisis, his sister Dora, who has recently moved to Paris, comes to the rescue. Although they had been estranged after the death of their mother in November 1930, their presence in Paris as exiles leads to a rapprochement, so much so that Dora allows Benjamin to stay in her apartment while she is away from Paris. During the summer, Benjamin visits Brecht in Denmark and experiences a respite from the difficulties of surviving in Paris. He stays with Brecht until late October when he returns to Paris. After a few days, he leaves for San Remo, Italy, where he stays at the boarding house owned by Dora, his former wife. After the bitterness of their divorce in 1930, Benjamin and Dora re-establish contact. Benjamin stays in San Remo through the winter of 1934–35 – a situation he describes as nesting "in the ruins of my own past" (*C*, 465). While he complains of the intellectual isolation of San Remo, these months allow him to work on his notes for the Arcades Project. He also sees his son Stefan again after a gap of almost two years. Stefan, now sixteen years old, had stayed on in school in Berlin and then in Vienna after Dora's move to Italy.

The year 1935 sees Benjamin developing closer links to the Institute for Social Research which has now moved to New York. The Institute commissions two essays from Benjamin. The first is entitled "Problems in the Sociology of Language," the second "Eduard Fuchs, Collector and Historian." Benjamin also produces a written account of the goals of his Arcades Project in a text known as the "Exposé of 1935." While working on this exposé, Benjamin recognizes the larger significance of this project. For the first time, he speaks of it as a book whose purpose will be to "unfold the nineteenth century from the perspective of France." The "Exposé" is enthusiastically received by Adorno, who advocates on Benjamin's behalf for financial support from the Institute. With Horkheimer's agreement, Benjamin receives a stipend. Although this support is intended to help Benjamin make progress with the Arcades Project, Benjamin turns to other new projects this year, notably his essay "The Storyteller" and, more importantly, his most famous work, "The Work of Art in the Age of Its Technical Reproducibility." While Adorno praises some aspects of the work of art essay, he is also critical, especially concerning areas where he sees the undue influence of Brecht's Marxism on Benjamin. Despite this criticism, their friendship grows until they finally move to a first name basis in 1936. After they meet in Paris this year, Benjamin reports to Horkheimer that they share "a unanimity of views in regard to the most important theoretical concerns" (*GB* 5, 390). Given Benjamin's need of the Institute for financial support as well as a publishing venue, it is difficult to discern just how much overstatement there may be in this remark. The ease with which Benjamin acquiesces to the cutting of almost a third of his "Work of Art" essay when it is prepared in a French translation for publication in the Institute's journal indicates a pragmatism overruling any sustained defense of his own theoretical concerns.

In addition to ongoing negotiations with the Institute about his work, Benjamin also faces increasing difficulty surviving in Paris. Beginning with his stay in his sister's apartment in 1935, Benjamin will reside in six different locations between then and 1938 – apartments, hotels, even a *chambre de bonne* for four months at the end of 1937. Only at the beginning of 1938 does this constant displacement promise to relent when, in January, Benjamin signs a lease for an apartment at 10 rue Dombasle. This will be his last residence in Paris before attempting to flee Europe in 1940. This period will also see seven trips to San Remo. It is there, in December 1937, that he will see his son Stefan as well as Adorno and his wife Gretel for the last time. Already in exile in England, the Adornos will shortly leave for America.

The summer of 1938, spent with Brecht in Denmark, provides Benjamin a final respite from the gathering tensions in Europe. He makes use of this interlude to complete the essay "The Paris of the Second Empire in Baudelaire." However, with the arrival of fall, events in Europe produce an increasingly hostile situation for him. In October, Benjamin writes: "I do not know how long it will continue to be physically possible to breathe European air; after the events of the past weeks, it is spiritually impossible even now" (*C*, 575).

Benjamin is referring to Chamberlain's appeasement of Hitler in the Munich Agreement of September 1938. As if the political situation were not difficult enough, upon his return to Paris he finds out that his sister, already ill with a spinal cord disease, has been diagnosed with advanced arteriosclerosis. He also hears that his brother Georg has been transferred to another prison, which is better news than it seems since the real danger is a transfer to a concentration camp. The only good news is that Stefan and Dora have left Mussolini's Italy for the safety of London. In France, his political situation is also becoming precarious. Faced with an impending law that would abolish the right of asylum for foreigners in France, Benjamin initiates a request for French citizenship – a request that may be no more than a futile exercise. As he notes, "the decline of the rule of law in Europe makes any kind of legalization appear deceptive" (*C*, 578). His need for some kind of legalization becomes pressing in May 1939 when his German citizenship is revoked at the request of the Gestapo. Stateless, Benjamin's request for French citizenship takes on even greater significance. However, it will provide no escape. Benjamin's request is still in process at the time of his death almost two years later.

On top of all the difficulties Benjamin faces on his return to Paris, he receives a discouraging response from the Institute regarding his Baudelaire essay. Adorno informs Benjamin that the essay should not be published in its present form. Benjamin has little choice but to rewrite it. This revision produces "On Some Motifs in Baudelaire" which is published by the Institute in 1940. Adorno praises the revision unsparingly, telling Benjamin that "it is the most perfect thing you have done since the book on *Trauerspiel* [Origin of the German Tragic Drama] and the essay on Kraus"(*AB*, 319). Yet, Adorno still has criticisms, particularly about the discussion of "aura" in the revision, a concept Adorno feels is still "incompletely thought out." These criticisms already signal Benjamin's methodological differences with the Frankfurt School, differences that become even more pronounced in the set of theses on history he will complete in spring 1940. The theses are notable for Benjamin's willingness to combine historical materialism and dialectical thought with theological ideas, notably the messianic. This work, not published until after his death, is regarded by Benjamin as not only a summation of the different strands of thought present in his work but an explosive one.

After the German invasion of Poland in September 1939, Benjamin along with other German and Austrian nationals is interned at the Olympic stadium in Paris. After ten days, a group including Benjamin is transferred to a work camp near Nevers. The internees suffer harsh conditions which greatly aggravate Benjamin's heart condition as well as the depressive state to which he has frequently succumbed during his last years. Benjamin remains at Nevers for almost three months and is only released when a friend, Adrienne Monnier, enlists the help of a French diplomat, Henri Hoppenot. Upon his release, Benjamin turns again to securing an escape from Europe. His decision is fraught with conflict. He writes to Horkheimer: "There is no need for me to tell you of the extent to which I feel myself attached to France, as much by friendships as by my work. For me, nothing in the world could replace the Bibliothèque Nationale" (*GB* 6, 373). Here, Benjamin again displays a disinclination to making hasty decisions despite the threat that surrounds him. His former wife, Dora, who has visited Paris at the beginning of 1940, tries to convince him to go to London but to no avail. In the end, as in 1933, when Gretel Adorno insisted that Benjamin leave Berlin, Benjamin's decision is again precipitated by the action of friends rather than by his own resolve.

1940 Flight from Europe

The real risk would be not to go.

The invasion of Belgium and the Netherlands in May leads to another round of internments in France. But this time Benjamin is spared, again thanks to the help of Adrienne Monnier's diplomat friend. This reprieve gives Benjamin the opportunity to arrange the safekeeping of his important papers. Georges Bataille receives all the materials relating to his research on the Arcades Project as well as other manuscripts. These papers will be kept safe at the Bibliothèque Nationale for the duration of the war.

Faced with the deteriorating situation in Europe and in failing health, Benjamin leaves Paris for Lourdes in mid-June along with his sister Dora. Lourdes offers a haven, but at a price. The altitude at Lourdes worsens both of their medical ailments. Contact with friends is difficult. Furthermore, the establishment of the Vichy government in July also brings with it the fear that a law abolishing asylum for foreigners will now be enforced. Benjamin's situation becomes more desperate. He contemplates going to Switzerland, a possibility that is still fraught with risk for a German Jew. Finally, in early August, he receives the news that the Institute has secured a visa for him to enter the United States. Benjamin travels to Marseilles in order to pick up his visa from the American Consulate. However, he still lacks the necessary exit visa from France. Without this, the other papers are useless. Benjamin stays in Marseilles for over a month in the hope of receiving the exit visa. His letters from Marseilles tell of his deep depression as he recognizes that he has no chance of obtaining the exit visa. In September he takes the train from Marseilles to Banyuls-sur-Mer, a small town close to the Spanish border, in the company of two friends who also intend to cross the Pyrenees into Spain. Although there is uncertainty as to the precise date when the crossing takes place, the group appears to have explored the route on September 25. After following part of the path towards Spain, Benjamin's companions return to town with Lisa Fittko, whose husband Benjamin had met while interned in France. Benjamin, fearful that his medical condition will prevent him from completing the crossing if he were to return to Banyuls-sur-Mer, insists on waiting for them to rejoin him the next morning. On September 26, the party reaches Port Bou on the Spanish side, only to discover that the border has been closed to refugees who lack an exit visa from France. As a result of this closing, the Spanish authorities inform them that they will be returned to France the following morning. That night, in a hotel in Port Bou, Benjamin takes an overdose of morphine tablets he has kept in his possession since leaving Paris. His death is recorded in the Port Bou register as occurring at 10 p.m. on September 26, 1940.

There are inconsistencies in the official records of what happened on September 26–27. These inconsistencies, along with the disappearance of the briefcase he was carrying – including a manuscript to which he attached great importance – have fueled much speculation about the nature of his death as well as precisely what the briefcase contained. In all likelihood, the manuscript was a final copy of the "Theses on the Concept of History" and not a completed manuscript of *The Arcades Project*. Speculation that it was the latter probably has more to do with the mythical status this project has attained in the decades after his death.

Benjamin's death in 1940 is followed by the death of his brother, Georg, in 1942 at the Sachsenhausen concentration camp. He dies as a result of touching the electric fence surrounding the camp. Even though his death is reported as a suicide, his wife Hilde Benjamin (sister-in-law of Walter and future Minister of Justice in East Germany after the war) states in her 1978 biography of Georg that he was driven to his death. His sister, Dora, is interned in a camp in the Pyrenees after his departure for Marseilles. She later escapes to Switzerland and lives out the war in Zurich before dying in 1946 from the spinal cord disease she had contracted in 1935. After moving to London, Benjamin's former wife, Dora, enters a marriage of convenience in order to establish rights of residency. Her new husband disappears immediately after the marriage. As she had done in San Remo, Dora runs several boarding houses in the Notting Hill district. She dies in May 1964. Benjamin's son, Stefan, is interned in Australia during the war. Once the war is over, he returns to London and completes a university degree. He subsequently works as a bookseller until his death in February 1972 at the age of fifty-four. Stefan has two daughters, the only direct descendants of Walter Benjamin. Both live in the United Kingdom, where one teaches English and the other works in film.

Chapter 2

Contexts

The principal contexts relevant to the development of Walter Benjamin's work are not simply historical or intellectual but are frequently a combination of both. Yet, despite this crossing over, the following historical contexts can be distinguished: the First World War, the rise and collapse of the Weimar Republic, and the seizure of power by the Nazis in 1933. On the intellectual side, the most significant contexts are provided by the student youth and school reform movements during his school and early university years, the George Circle which was the reigning critical school in Germany during Benjamin's formative critical years, and the context provided by both Bertolt Brecht's Marxism and the Institute for Social Research – or as it is more familiarly known, the Frankfurt School.

The student youth movement and the First World War

The social and political organization of Germany at the beginning of the twentieth century offered little to its youth. Ruled by a Kaiser, Wilhelm II, Germany was a heavily autocratic society defined by the conservative and nationalist ideals of its ruling class. Conformism to these ideals left no room for individual expression nor did it provide any significant political role for the middle class. The German youth movement, a purely middle-class phenomenon that sought to cultivate the natural tendencies of youth, arose from this vacuum.

The beginnings of this movement can be traced to 1901. It was formed in a suburb of Berlin very similar to the ones in which Benjamin spent his childhood. From its beginnings as a neighborhood organization that took the name *Wandervogel* ("bird of passage" – a name intended to catch the move-ment's emphasis on freedom as well as collective excursions), it spread to most major German cities by 1906. As a movement, however, the *Wandervogel* had no uniform goals. Different groups and sects with different interests appeared. But what they all offered was the opportunity of an alternative experience away from the rigidity of German society. As the youth movement developed between 1906 and 1914, various groupings emerged: some focused on school reform, others sought greater social and political engagement. By 1914, a feder-ation of youth movements had emerged under the name Free German Youth; it had approximately 60,000 members at this time.

Benjamin's contact with this movement began in 1905 when he attended a progressive boarding school where Gustav Wyneken, a noted proponent of youth, was a teacher (see chapter 1). Wyneken rejected the romanticizing character of the *Wandervogel*. In its place he sought to cultivate the natural tendencies of youth as the basis of a program to change society as a whole. Central to his thinking was the idea of "youth culture." Rather than form a transition between childhood and adulthood, Wyneken held that youth was a stage with its own specific characteristics and expressiveness. In addition, for him, the task of education was to develop this stage and not stifle it with adult models or conservative views of school curriculum. Benjamin's early essays reflected Wyneken's ideas – many of which were published in the journal associated with Wyneken, *Der Anfang*.

In 1914, the idealism of youth movement lends itself easily to involvement in the First World War. Caught up in the enthusiasm exhibited for war by the youth movement, Benjamin and his friends try to enlist. But after the double suicide of two of his friends from the student youth group Benjamin belonged to in Berlin, he not only breaks with Wyneken on account of his support of the war but also with the youth movement.

The George School

During the first decades of the twentieth century, the single most influential literary school in Germany developed around the poet Stefan George (1868–1933). The circle had two purposes: to serve as a means for George to cultivate himself as a mythical poetic figure, and to create a vision of Germany. This vision was embodied in what Karl Wolfskehl, a senior member of George's circle, referred to in 1910 as "the *secret Germany*, the only one alive in our time, which has found expression here, only here . . . Of all the peoples of Europe, we Germans are the only ones who have not yet fulfilled themselves."[1] The idea of such a Germany sustained the George Circle and also informed the writings, both critical and literary, produced by its members. Overseeing these writings, George exerted an autocratic power that sought to shape both the literary past and present of Germany. This circle provided the dominant critical context for Benjamin as he began his career as a literary critic.

At its height, the George Circle's dominance was so great that it eclipsed the literary and historical scholarship of the universities. A massive, 800-page study of Goethe, published by Friedrich Gundolf, one of George's closest disciples, not only went through three editions within a year; by 1931, 50,000 copies were in print. This influential book became the target of Benjamin's attack on the George Circle in his essay "Goethe's *Elective Affinities*." With this attack, Benjamin's intention was clearly to wrest criticism away from the orthodoxy demanded by the George Circle while exposing the critical vacuity of its exemplary works.

After the war, the George Circle still held a place of prominence despite the defection of followers and the tyrannical exclusion of Gundolf in 1920 when he announced to George that he would marry. George's autocratic style and his unceasing desire to create himself as the leader through whom the cultural renewal of Germany would take place was, in the end, the undoing of the circle and its influence. After he died in 1933, his significance quickly waned. Although the Nazis had co-opted him for his rhetoric of national self-renewal and had celebrated his death by establishing a literary prize in his name, they quickly allowed him to drop from sight on account of the homoerotic character of his circle as well as his significant inclusion of Jewish members. Nonetheless, George's sense of national spiritual renewal was hard to distinguish from Nazi rhetoric. At one point, George himself went so far as to credit himself for the rise of Nazism when he stated: "I absolutely do not deny being the forefather of the new national movement."[2] In the end, the importance of the George Circle died with its master. Even now it is little studied despite its extensive influence in Germany in the first decades of the twentieth century.

The Weimar Republic and the rise of National Socialism

The Weimar Republic is the name given to the liberal democracy that arose in 1919 and lasted until Hitler seized power in 1933. The existence of the Weimar Republic correlates approximately with the years in which Benjamin attempts to establish himself in Germany, first in the university system, and then as a critic. These are years marked by extremes: a virtual civil war between communists and conservatives immediately after the First World War; hyper-inflation in the early 1920s; a flourishing in culture, art, music, social and political philosophy, and architecture; and finally, the rise of a totalitarian force in the form of National Socialism.

The Republic is named after Weimar because the national assembly, fearful of the violence that had affected Berlin, held its first meeting there after the 1919 elections. Despite the election of a governing assembly, conflict and unrest continue. In April 1919, a Soviet republic is declared in Munich but is subsequently put down by government troops. In March 1920, an attempted putsch occurs in Berlin. The government flees to Stuttgart and calls for a general strike, which causes the putsch to fail. The general strike, however, precipitates communist rebellions in other parts of Germany. These events surface in Benjamin's 1921 essay "The Critique of Violence," when he considers the critical significance of the general strike. This period of strife, which lasts until 1923, and the split between the Social Democrats and the Communists not only makes governing Germany difficult but greatly weakens the economy. Already crippled by war and the reparations demanded by the allies, Germany experiences inflation on a colossal scale. By November 1923, 1$ is worth 4.2 trillion marks. Paper currency is a cheaper form of home heating than firewood. This same month marks the first significant appearance of Hitler on the political scene with the attempt to seize power in the unsuccessful "beer-hall" putsch in Munich. The putsch is successfully put down and Hitler is imprisoned, if only for a short period. By late 1923, the Social Democrats form a controlling coalition in government and usher in a period of relative calm which lasts until 1928. The economy recovers, and the artistic and cultural flourish with which Weimar is most frequently associated comes to the fore.

Berlin in the 1920s became the focus of the European avant-garde. Modernism in art, music, literature, and architecture and design thrived in an atmosphere of experimentation fostered by technological advances in cinema as well as by the influence of new intellectual vistas opened by psychoanalysis, expressionism, and social and political theory. Dramatists such as Bertolt Brecht emerged, and composers such as Arnold Schoenberg, Alban Berg, and Brecht's collaborator Kurt Weill; novelists such as Thomas Mann, Alfred Döblin, and Hermann Hesse; artists such as Wassily Kandinsky and Paul Klee; filmmakers such as Fritz Lang, F. W. Murnau, Ernst Lubitsch, and Josef von Sternberg; actresses such as Marlene Dietrich and Pola Negri; intellectual figures such as Carl Jung, Erich Fromm, Sigmund Freud, Georg Lukács, and Siegfried Kracauer; and architects such as Walter Gropius and Mies van der Rohe – not to mention the various artistic movements that either emerged in Berlin or, like Dada and Bauhaus, eventually found their way there.

The artistic and cultural achievements of the Weimar Republic take place in a relatively short period. The high point is reached by 1928. After this date, another period of political instability begins. In addition to the international economic crisis of 1929 and the resulting high unemployment rate, the death of Gustav Stresemann, who had helped guide Germany from 1923 to 1929, decreases greatly the ability of the Weimar democracy to deal with the economic and political challenges it now faces. This situation sets the scene for the re-emergence of Hitler. In the 1930 elections, the Nazi Party makes significant gains by exploiting both the economic situation and the collapse of the governing coalition formed by the Social Democrats with more conservative elements. But what is historically important for Germany in the next few years is that this election ushers in a period of paralyzed government in which no single party has a majority and no coalition is possible.

During this time, the Nazis mount a relentless campaign aimed at undermining the Weimar constitution while simultaneously using it to protect their own gains. In the elections of July 1932 increased political violence occurs as Hitler's uniformed SA troops fight street battles with the communists – battles that played into the hands of his electoral strategy by raising fear among the middle class. The inconclusive results from these elections again result in a paralyzed parliament. Of greater significance, however, is the growth of the paramilitary force the Nazis have at their control during these years. Consisting of over 400,000 members by 1932, it exerts large-scale intimidation as the Nazis strengthen their position in Germany. This intimidation cuts Benjamin off from one of his few sources of economic support: the broadcasts he performs for the Berlin and Frankfurt radio stations. In this same year, the Nazis exploit the parliamentary paralysis and move to have Hitler appointed Chancellor. Unable to resolve the crisis in government any other way, and only after Hitler makes a specious pledge to uphold the constitution, does Hindenberg, then President, appoint Hitler to the Chancellorship. Hitler is sworn in on January 30, 1933. Shortly afterwards, in March 1933, Benjamin leaves Berlin for Paris and never returns. By August 1934, the Nazis have gained total power in Germany.

Marxism and the Frankfurt School

Benjamin's first direct experience with Marxism begins with his reading of Lukács's *History and Class Consciousness* in 1924. This exposure, along with the influence of Asja Lacis, sets in motion the political turn that finds increased expression in his work in the late 1920s. In 1929, these first influences are given a stronger push after he meets Bertolt Brecht. Brecht's sway over Benjamin continues in the 1930s; however, the social and political criticism of the Frankfurt School also begins to exert an influence, principally through the figure of Theodor Adorno. In 1928, Benjamin begins a dialogue with Adorno that develops significantly through the 1930s. As this dialogue develops, it becomes clear that Benjamin is not only caught between these two quite different accounts of how Marx is to be interpreted for contemporary social and political experience but also caught between two personalities that have little sympathy for each other.

Through his reading of Lukács, Benjamin is introduced to historical materialism. This approach sees history in terms of the material conditions of existence rather than from the ideological positions promoted by the controlling classes of a society. Using these conditions to expose and also critique the ideology at work in those positions initiates a project that aims at a fundamental recasting of what history is. No longer an ideological narrative, history is now based on the material evidence of how a society or culture is organized and on how political and economic forces are mediated by that evidence. Brecht and the Frankfurt School explicitly pose the question contained in this approach, namely: by what means can the critique produced by historical materialism have a productive effect on contemporary social and political conditions?

As a dramatist and theater producer, Brecht seeks a direct answer to this question. The "alienation effect" (*Verfremdungseffekt*) is the most well-known technique explored by Brecht as a means of experiencing the material conditions under which art and culture are produced. Less well known is another concept, "re-functioning" (*Umfunktionierung*), which Benjamin will use in his essay "The Author as Producer." The purpose of this concept in Brecht is to transform existing media such as theater, opera, etc., so that their use of illusion no longer functions as a means of sustaining institutions (social and political) or of maintaining an exclusively "culinary" attitude towards art (as something to be digested). Instead, a re-functioned art effects social change by making spectators in the theater experience and then judge their contemporary situation rather than sacrifice judgment to an empathy with what happens on stage. For Brecht, the goal of this re-functioning is "to convert . . . institutions from places of entertainment into organs of mass communication."[3]

The difference between Brecht and the Frankfurt School lay in a different understanding of how social change was to be produced. Brecht sought a more direct means of change by involving the segment of society that had most to benefit. For Adorno, this approach was an example of the reductive thinking exhibited by vulgar Marxism. In contrast, the Frankfurt School remained committed to the intellectual development of critique as a source of social and political change.

The School is formed in Frankfurt in February 1923 under the official title of Institute for Social Research. However, it is not until 1930, when Max Horkheimer becomes director, that it begins to achieve the reputation for which it is now known. Other major figures associated with the Institute in the 1920s and 1930s include Theodor Adorno, Friedrich Pollock, Leo Löwenthal, Herbert Marcuse, Siegfried Kracauer, and Erich Fromm. Although supported by and published by the Institute in the 1930s, Benjamin retains a distinct individual voice against the more collective approach shared, in particular, by the Institute's two strongest voices: Adorno and Horkheimer.

The Institute engages with the difficulty of working within Marxist categories under historical conditions quite different from those experienced by Marx. This engagement leads to a reconceiving of Marxism in the light of historical forces and configurations that classical Marxism does not and cannot account for. In this respect, neo-Marxist is a better description of the Institute's work. A central aspect of this neo-Marxist approach is what is known as "Critical Theory." This approach possesses no uniform method; rather, it announces a type of inquiry that seeks to intervene in the social and historical conditions of contemporary experience. This intervention occurs through the critical attitude maintained by the Institute's theoretical approaches. Such an attitude is necessary because existence is governed by changing social and historical forces rather than a fixed rational truth. In order to counter these forces, theory has to be critical. For the Institute this means that critical theory has to be oriented towards emancipation; otherwise, it will remain politically and socially ineffective. While Benjamin clearly shares these goals – and Brecht too – their different understanding of how to produce such goals also reveals the difficulty faced by the Frankfurt School: critique makes such goals significant but these same goals are not necessarily realizable through critique.

Chapter 3

Works

(a) Metaphysical beginnings 1914–1918

In the writings presented in this section, Benjamin moves away from the education and school reform subjects to which his earliest writings have been devoted. Concerns that now appear include the nature of language and the poetic, as well as the relation of history and criticism. Four essays written by Benjamin between 1914 and 1918 are emphasized here: "The Life of Students"; "Two Poems by Friedrich Hölderlin"; "On Language in General and on the Language of Man"; and "On the Program of the Coming Philosophy." The first of these works is written when he is just twenty-two years old; the last is completed when he is twenty-six and about to begin work on his doctoral dissertation. Only the first of these essays appears in print during Benjamin's lifetime. Despite not being published, the remaining essays are recognized for the place they hold as early developments of issues that will later receive more critical and less metaphysically inclined treatment.

"The Life of Students" (1914–1915, pub. 1915)

> Our concern here must be with inner unity, not with critique from outside.

Benjamin's essay "The Life of Students" shows the influence of the ideas and hopes of the student reform movement he first experienced during his school years. The idealism of the student youth movement, so evident in Benjamin's earliest writings on education, is still present in this essay but in a way that registers difficulties within the contemporary German university, particularly with regard to its emphasis on the vocational training of students. Within such a university, Benjamin argues, the kind of education most appropriate to students cannot take place: the education that fosters a progressive spirit of independent thinking. Even where there is an appearance of independence, Benjamin remarks that the three elements most essential to independence and a progressive spirit are missing: "radical doubt, fundamental critique, and the most important thing of all – the life that would be willing to dedicate itself to reconstruction – are excluded" (*SW* 1, 41). While "life" is given the greatest emphasis here, the importance of critique cannot be underestimated. Earlier in the essay, Benjamin proclaims that "the only possibility" for the modern university student "is to liberate the future from the deformations of the present by an act of cognition. For this, criticism alone serves" (*SW* 1, 38). Already present here is the extent to which criticism will figure in Benjamin's thinking as a crucial means of safeguarding and revealing whatever has the greatest significance. Such a criticism is the pathway to the "only possibility" Benjamin can envisage for the university if it is to avoid perverting the "creative spirit" of youth into the vocational spirit. For Benjamin, this possibility turns on a sense of "inner unity" for student life. But, to grasp this inner unity, the university must be criticized from the inside rather than from an external position. By adopting this kind of criticism, known as immanent criticism, Benjamin already advocates a critical practice that not only will be fundamental to the Frankfurt School but also will underwrite the critical task explored in much of his subsequent writing.

Benjamin's deployment of this critical practice against the university takes aim at what passes for knowledge within academic study at that time. Remarks such as the following are particularly biting: "the only remarkable and even astounding point to be emphasized here is the extent to which institutes of higher learning are characterized by a gigantic game of hide-and-seek in which students and teachers, each in his or her own unified identity, constantly push past one another without ever seeing one another" (*SW* 1, 39). Because of the prevalence of this game, what is missing, for Benjamin, is "life" and "a community of learning."

Benjamin associates both of these terms with what he calls "direct creativity." The value placed on this creativity is enormous since it characterizes the notion of life Benjamin privileges in this essay. At the same time, this creativity defines life in terms of a general productivity that includes not only artistic production but also teaching and learning – the latter two elements being precisely what the modern university has deformed. By relating all three of these elements to creativity, Benjamin seeks to gather them in a way that expresses their unity. Yet, creativity is not the source of the "inner unity" Benjamin has spoken of before. This inner unity is now identified as nothing less than love: "the ability to love ... must be the source of [the student's] creativity" (*SW* 1, 42). This turn to love is perhaps a surprising one in an essay whose critical focus takes aim at the teaching and learning of a university that has eliminated creativity under the weight of vocational training. Yet, in the context of the student reform movement, which influenced greatly Benjamin's thinking about education, love figures as a prized possession of youth (note Benjamin's pseudonym from his school days, "Ardor"). When Benjamin attributes the creative forces that are the particular property of youth to love, he not only adheres to this context but also reveals the extent to which his critical thinking is directed towards justifying a unity for both intellectual and social situations.

Love is then the element that defines and distinguishes "the community of creative human beings" for Benjamin. Its effect, however, is not restricted to such a community. The community created through love, Benjamin continues, "elevates every field of study to the universal through the form of philosophy" (*SW* 1, 42–43). Community and philosophy are closely linked here, but only because such a philosophy is not concerned with technical philosophical issues. Benjamin explains, it is concerned with "the great metaphysical questions of Plato and Spinoza, the Romantics, and Nietzsche" (*SW* 1, 43). Philosophy in this sense offers Benjamin what he describes as the "closest links between life and the professions." In his words, this is "a life more deeply conceived" (*SW* 1, 43).

This deeper conception of life is based on a love that to this point has had an abstract existence – as if it had no relation to Eros. For Benjamin, the separation of love and Eros has also been a failing of university life. By deforming the creativity Benjamin traces to love, the university has been the setting in which the erotic aspect of love has been repressed. Benjamin locates this repression in the affinity between the university and what he names the "bourgeois conventions" that instill expectations of marriage and the founding of a family. Even the much heralded freedom of university students is seen by Benjamin as yet another example of how true Eros has been neutralized by a false sense of the erotic gained from prostitution. Despite such an example, this is not a matter restricted to male students. In Benjamin's eyes, it affects both men and women.

Benjamin offers a notion of community as a means of countering this neutralization of a true Eros. In doing so, it is clear that his understanding of community is one that seeks to include men and women in an equal way within the university. Benjamin writes: "To transform the necessary independence of the creative spirit and to bring about the necessary inclusion of women, who are not productive in a masculine sense, in a single community of creative persons – through love – this indeed is the goal to which students should aspire, because it is the form of their own lives" (*SW* 1, 44). The forces that work against the creation of such a community are located in the bourgeois views of intellectual social life that the university has affirmed rather than provided the means to criticize. While Benjamin's analysis of the university and its students remains idealistic as well as metaphysical in its concern with an inner unity presented through love, there are aspects of this analysis that already point towards concerns that will surface in later works. The historical understanding through which Benjamin sees the university and its students is one of these.

The introductory paragraph to "The Life of Students" already hints at such an understanding. After describing one view of history as "advance along the path of progress," Benjamin offers another view that delineates "a particular condition in which history happens to be concentrated in a single focal point" (*SW* 1, 37). Readers already familiar with a text Benjamin was working on at the very end of his life may recall similar remarks. In "On the Concept of History" (1940), Benjamin criticizes history as progress and does so in the name of a "present . . . in which time has come to a standstill" (*SW* 4, 396). While these two views may share a formal similarity since both oppose any understanding of history as progress, Benjamin interprets this concentration of history in a distinctly different way at the beginning of his career – it is not the political, materialist, and messianic interpretation he offers later.

In "The Life of Students" Benjamin first compares this single focal point to what has "traditionally been found in the utopian images of the philosophers" (*SW* 1, 37). He then goes on to say, "The historical task is to disclose this immanent state of perfection and make it absolute, to make it visible and dominant in the present" (*SW* 1, 37). This remark reveals how much Benjamin's thinking remains within the idealist and metaphysical concerns that guide him at this time. Yet, there is also a strong drive to develop a basis for criticism from within these concerns. Benjamin rejects the use of an external idea or reference point for such a basis. Instead, it is drawn from within the present state of university life – an idealism rooted in the actuality of the present and articulated through youth's capacity for love. What emerges from this position, when considered alongside the essay on Hölderlin, also written at this time, is the strong sense Benjamin already possesses of the modern as what demands engagement with a task. Here, it is the historical task. In the Hölderlin essay, it is the critical task. To accept the modern and its significance already appears in these early essays as an acceptance of the demands made by such tasks.

"Two Poems by Friedrich Hölderlin" (1914–1915)

The poetized is identical with life.

This essay is Benjamin's first substantial work on a literary topic. The intention of the essay is obscured by its prosaic title. What Benjamin undertakes is less an interpretation of the German Romantic poet Friedrich Hölderlin – whose poetry had recently been rescued from obscurity by the George School (see chapter 2) – than an account of the inner form of the poetic as it is exemplified in two poems by Hölderlin. The close relation of this essay to the piece on "The Life of Students" is evident here: where the latter has sought to make present the "inner unity" of the intellectual and social life of students, this aspect is now complemented in the realm of literature by what Benjamin calls "inner form." At the outset, this task of presenting "inner form" may seem a familiar one if a sense of form as something distinct from content is applied. Unfortunately, this does not apply, because Benjamin understands inner form as the content of the poem. In a tradition that has kept form and content resolutely separate from one another, this claim will seem confusing. The question posed by this essay is how the inner form of a poem can also be its content.

Already, it should be clear that Benjamin's aesthetic commentary will be no effusive outpouring about the poetic spirit or the beauty of poetry's aesthetic qualities. To grasp what he is attempting here first requires an understanding of precisely what he is not doing. In this respect, Benjamin can be our guide: "Nothing will be said here about the process of lyrical composition, nothing about the person or world view of the creator" (*SW* 1, 18). If inner form is not related to the process of composition, and if it is not related to any external source such as an author's world view, then what Benjamin introduces in this essay is a claim about poetry that goes beyond the methods that have prevailed in literary interpretation. Such a claim was also shared by what was known at this time as the George School, a literary group formed around the early twentieth-century German lyric poet Stefan George. George's influence on literary study is in many respects the result of a carefully calculated creation of himself as a poetic leader. That this persona developed by George appealed to the young Benjamin is evident from the end of "The Life of Students" when he cites one of George's poems as an example of the kind of insight that student life is alienated from. The counter to this alienation will again be life; however, under the influence of George this sense of life will insist on poetry as an autonomous creation whose aesthetic significance lies in its inner form, its freedom from external sources of meaning. Yet, at the same time, Benjamin aims at something more than the aesthetics of the George School. Although adopting the form of an aesthetic commentary, Benjamin explores an understanding of literature that is at once more philosophical in character and more serious with respect to the significance of literature.

This seriousness about the status and importance of poetic language marks Benjamin's essay as a distinctive attempt to grasp precisely what the "poetic task" is. The elaboration of this task produces an extremely dense piece of writing that makes little concession to its readers in either the difficulty of its concepts or its exposition (the essay is strongly recursive and full of passive verb forms). While the question of Benjamin's writing style will be addressed in the context of later work, suffice it to say for now that Benjamin already reveals in this essay a tendency towards a compacted style of thinking that is at odds with a more logical and expository presentation.

Elaborating what the poetic task is turns upon a question of method: how is the properly poetic aspect of a poem to be justified without resorting to external causes or explanations such as those offered by history, society, politics, and so on? In answering this question, Benjamin presents the poetic task as something that occurs in a unique and singular way in every poem. As such, the actual reading of a work remains unavoidable for Benjamin – hence the rather prosaic title of this essay, "Two Poems by Friedrich Hölderlin."

For Benjamin, the relation of life to the work of art is at the center of the poetic. What is at stake in this relation is not a single idea – he would consider this a denial of life. Rather, what is at stake is a "sphere of relation." This sphere of relation, Benjamin states, is the inner form of a poem. Within this sphere, life and the work of art exist in a unity. This unity is not a static relation or point of reference (this would also be a denial of life). A different notion of unity is at work here, one rooted in life. What this means emerges from some of Benjamin's remarks on life.

Benjamin first writes that life cannot yield how it is unified and then goes on to assert that, because of this, the unities of life "are wholly ungraspable." Important here is that Benjamin does not question the role of "ungraspable" unities in his understanding of the poetic. Indeed, he clearly argues that they must remain ungraspable. Furthermore, no attempt should be made to reveal the ungraspable: "the disclosure of the pure poetized, the absolute task, must remain . . . a purely methodological, ideal goal" (*SW* 1, 20–21). What Benjamin means here is that the ideal, by being ungraspable, justifies an understanding of the poetic based on relations between life and work that are far from ideal. In other words, it is impossible to exhaust all the possible ways in which life and work may be related to one another. If this were not the case, there could only be one poem, an ideal poem. If the ideal is always ungraspable, then a poem cannot reach it. As a result, a poem must be content with the relation to life it presents – precisely because no other relation is possible for it when the ideal is ungraspable. Since its ideal is the ungraspable, the poem belongs to life.

The metaphysical aspect of Benjamin's thinking in this essay appears in his reliance on an unquestioned ideal. While such a reliance will be relinquished in his later thought, it is evoked in this context as the means by which the uniqueness of every poem is justified. By making the ideal ungraspable (giving it life in Benjamin's terms), the poem becomes an individual expression. If every poem were the expression of an ideal, this would not be possible because poetry would then lack any distinguishing property. Every poem would just be a form expressing the same idea. By removing the ideal from the poetic, Benjamin is attempting to account for why a poem is able to express more than one meaning. A poetry possessing this ability is for Benjamin a poetry that provides an expression of life. Since inner form is what assures such an expression, it is the properly poetic element in poetry.

Benjamin's task in this essay is to establish the significance of the poetic without recourse to an external source of meaning, whether this is found in the social context of the poem or the life of the author, or in some ideal. Yet, as Benjamin expresses his understanding of the poetic, he does not altogether relinquish the ideal – after all, he does say that it remains a methodological necessity. As a result something beyond our intellectual and perceptual relation to the poetic remains in force. Recognizing that this ideal cannot be grasped by the poetic, Benjamin seeks to justify the evaluation and judgment of the poetic when the one thing that would affirm such judgment and evaluation remains ungraspable. This is emphatically stated in the sentence that ends the methodological section of this essay. Benjamin writes: "what will emerge more clearly, however, is that with respect to lyric poetry, a judgment, even if unprovable, can nonetheless be justified" (*SW* 1, 21). To justify judgment when the ideal cannot be grasped is the task of this essay. What is then at stake for Benjamin is a critical understanding of the poetic that does not transgress the limit surrounding the ideal. The kind of method Benjamin is using here belongs to immanent criticism, that is, a criticism whose focus remains resolutely fixed on the internal structure and presentation of an individual work. It is also a criticism that seeks its justification from that focus. The question Benjamin addresses by adopting such a method is the question of what justifies the existence and value of a work of art when external conditions cannot be called upon to fulfill this role. Raising this question begins an inquiry into the modern significance of art, which for Benjamin means a significance no longer determined by literary history and, above all else, no longer dominated by the idealist concept of poetry and literature that dominated German criticism through the figure of Goethe.

Suggested further reading

Rainer Nägele. "Benjamin's Ground." In *Benjamin's Ground*. Ed. Rainer Nägele. Detroit: Wayne State University Press, 1988. 19–38.
David Wellbery. "Benjamin's Theory of the Lyric." In *Benjamin's Ground*. Ed. Rainer Nägele. Detroit: Wayne State University Press, 1988. 39–59.

"On Language in General and on the Language of Man" (1916)

> All language communicates itself.

The title under which this essay is commonly known, "On Language as Such and on the Language of Man," is a little misleading. "On Language in General and on the Language of Man" gives a better sense of how Benjamin understands language in this essay. On the one hand, there is language that names – this is the language of man. On the other there is a more general sense of language, one that includes the language of man but which at the same time is "coextensive . . . with absolutely everything" (*SW* 1, 62). In the course of this essay, Benjamin is careful to keep his focus on the former because, for him, not to do so would be "to rob linguistic theory of its deepest insights" (*SW* 1, 64). What this essay aims at through such a focus is an account of naming not just as an expression of the "innermost nature of language itself" but also as the place where "the essential law of language appears" (*SW* 1, 65).

Of the three essays discussed from this period in Benjamin's writing, "On Language in General" is the most abstract and the most demanding. Its argument is dense and Benjamin's thought moves, at times, in such a compressed and recursive way that a first reading is more liable to bewilder than enlighten. Benjamin even admits to "the fragmentary nature of its ideas" in a letter from November 1916, but also asserts that despite this aspect there is "a systematic intent" to the essay (*C*, 82). Beyond the difficulties posed by its manner of exposition, "On Language in General" remains an important statement about a subject that will continue to have significance in Benjamin's thinking, particularly in "The Task of the Translator" and in his book *Origin of the German Tragic Drama*.

As if to counter the fragmentary nature of his ideas, Benjamin provides several indications about how to read this essay. His use of the word "language," he says, is "in no way metaphorical" (*SW* 1, 63) as it would be if the word were transposed into non-linguistic contexts – for example, in the phrase, "the language of painting." Benjamin's essay is, in this respect, a reflection on what language is, not what it can be represented as being. Benjamin also cautions against any understanding that would make language an abstraction lacking a relation to life and existence: "an existence entirely without relationship to language is an idea: but this idea can bear no fruit" (*SW* 1, 62). Together, language and existence are productive. However, once separated, existence becomes a mere idea, devoid of life, and thereby devoid of what is properly human about existence: the naming that occurs in human language, a naming through which the human communicates its existence.

Benjamin reinforces the distinction between language in general and human language by defining the latter as the expression of a "mental entity." By this Benjamin does not mean that language is simply a means of expressing mental activity such as thought and perception. Rather what Benjamin means is that human language and mental activity are inseparable from one another: to speak of language is also to speak of thought. The medium, language, and what it intends to convey are one and the same thing. Benjamin describes this state of affairs as a paradox and points to the Greek word "logos" as its example. Logos can mean both what is said, a word, and the medium in which it is said, language. For Benjamin, this paradox is at the center of linguistic theory; however, the paradox is not viewed as a challenge to such theory. Rather, it is seen as a solution.

By recognizing this paradox as the center of linguistic theory, Benjamin refuses the more normal expectation in such theoretical accounts, namely, emphasizing an idea or a concept in order to resolve the problems and issues posed by language. Such an idea, as Benjamin has already said, would bear no fruit. In its place, Benjamin aims at a productive theory of language, that is, a theory in which the productive force of language is recognized in the human ability to name.

Benjamin defines the role of the name in the following manner: "the name is that *through* which, and *in* which, language itself, and nothing more, com-municates itself absolutely" (*SW* 1, 63). Since, for Benjamin, language is the only thing that can communicate itself absolutely in language, naming is the way in which something that is purely language occurs. Already evident here is an understanding that refuses to accept that things existing in the world define what language is. When Benjamin presents the relation of language to an actual object, a lamp, he locates two ways in which the lamp exists, as object and as language: "The language of this lamp communicates, for example, not the lamp . . . but the language-lamp, the lamp in communication, the lamp in expression. For in language the situation is this: *the linguistic being of all things is their language*" (*SW* 1, 63). An obvious point, but one worth repeating here, is that the one thing language can never do is make an object appear as it is. What language communicates is not the object but the way that the object exists for language. Benjamin observes that this existence can only occur in the name. On one level, this does not appear to say very much. It is like saying that, in language, the lamp is a name. If we stay with this level of understanding, Benjamin is voicing nothing more than a tautology: what is said in language is language (because it is linguistic). Benjamin's phrase for this is "the linguistic being of all things is their language." Yet, Benjamin strongly asserts that what he is thinking is not a tautology. Why then is this understanding of language not tautological? And what then is its significance?

The phrase "the linguistic being of all things is their language" is not tautological for Benjamin because "'that which in a mental entity is communicable *is* its language.' On this 'is' (equivalent to 'is immediately') everything depends" (*SW* 1, 63). What this sentence says is that human language immediately communicates its ability to communicate. In distinction, a tautology says the same thing twice; it is a repetition ("a rose is a rose," etc.). This is not what Benjamin states here. What he states is that language, like the word logos, says two different things simultaneously. Furthermore, this ability to communicate does not depend on a speaker. Language has this property quite apart from any speaker. A crucial aspect of Benjamin's understanding of language emerges here. Language's ability to communicate is a property that belongs to language.

A first consequence of this understanding of language is that, quite apart from any consideration of what is being said or who is speaking, language always communicates that it is a means of communication. As a result, language is both a means and what is meant – precisely the property of the word logos mentioned previously. The effect of this for Benjamin is that one is immediately communicated in the other wherever language occurs. This is the property of language that Benjamin refers to in this essay as the "magic of language."

This sense of a "magic of language" offers a focus for Benjamin's thinking in this essay, but, in true Benjaminian fashion, this focus is not a simple one.

Benjamin gives another twist to his thinking when he says that what is magical about language is also the "primary problem of language" (*SW* 1, 64). What Benjamin had referred to as the solution of linguistic theory (the paradox of the word "logos") now turns out to be the fundamental problem in which the nature of language can be recognized.

Benjamin locates "the primary problem of language" in the ability of language to allow mediation and immediacy to occur simultaneously. His example of this is the role of language in communicating our mental existence. Benjamin argues that this existence cannot be communicated through language as if our mental existence were just like a thing or object existing in the world. This is so because mental existence is not a thing. Accordingly, the way we use language to represent other things in the world is not appropriate. If we were to view language as denoting only things, and if we say that our mental existence is represented in language, then, Benjamin argues, we would simply be claiming that our mental existence has the same relation to language as things. Nothing could be further from the truth for Benjamin. Instead of being communicated *through* language, mental existence is communicated *in* language. Since such existence is *in* language, Benjamin is saying that language mediates something that is also immediately present in language: "Because the mental being of man is language itself, man cannot communicate himself through it, but only in it" (*SW* 1, 65). The difference between "through" and "in" is perhaps the most difficult distinction this essay offers.

By emphasizing the ability of language to mediate something that is immediately present in language, Benjamin not only places a paradox at the very center of his theory but also insists upon an understanding of language that would rescue it from being seen as a mere means of representation. To restrict language to representation – a view Benjamin labels a "bourgeois conception of language" – denies language any productive role since it would always be tied to something else for its meaning. On this matter, Benjamin's position is uncompromisingly clear: "nothing is communicated *through* language" (*SW* 1, 64). But how then is communication *in* language productive? Benjamin goes on to say, "what is communicated *in* language cannot be externally limited or measured, and therefore all language contains its own incommensurable, uniquely constituted infinity. Its linguistic being, not its verbal contents, defines its frontier" (*SW* 1, 64). The only limit to the language Benjamin describes here is language itself, which means that it can have neither limit nor frontier imposed upon it. As a result, Benjamin concludes that such a language is infinite. In this infinite aspect the productive nature of language is found. Such a language, without anything to restrict it, is essentially free. And nowhere is this infinite, productive force of language more present for Benjamin than in the name.

To understand more about this productive force and how it occurs in the name, the magical aspect of language (the ability of language to be two things at once) must be recalled. When Benjamin first describes this twofold quality, he focuses on what occurs when names are used: "in name appears the essential law of language, according to which to express oneself and to address everything else amounts to the same thing" (*SW* 1, 65). The name performs both these functions without contradicting itself. Benjamin later reiterates this twofold quality in different terms when he states that "the word must communicate *something* (other than itself)" (*SW* 1, 71). Here, the word is understood to communicate both itself and something else.

Benjamin's emphasis on this twofold quality points to what is at stake in his understanding of language. Even though he insists on language as that which communicates itself, this communication cannot occur without a simultaneous, or immediate, address to something else. It is in this address that every thing that exists in the world has a name. And, by having a name, every thing in the world is known because of language. Benjamin summarizes this as follows: "All nature, insofar as it communicates itself, communicates itself in language" (*SW* 1, 65). In other words, if it were not for language, we would have no knowledge of the things that are in the world. The foundation of this knowledge is the name, since it is only in the name that things and objects can be communicated. This is what Benjamin describes when he refers to the "linguistic being of things" in this essay. It is not that things have language. Rather, it is because they do not have language that they are given a name by humans. For Benjamin, the name is both our relation to the world and our expression of that relation.

The ability to name that is so central to human language in Benjamin's theory also has a theological aspect. As Benjamin recalls, it is man who is given the task of naming by God. However, Benjamin explains, there is a difference between God's relation to names and names as they exist in human language. Benjamin writes, "God made things knowable in their names" (*SW* 1, 68). This describes the creative word of God in Genesis, for example in the phrase "let there be light." Accordingly, the word creates what it names (Benjamin says that their relation is identical). On the other hand, in human language, things are named "according to knowledge" (*SW* 1, 68). What this difference indicates is that human language is a reflection of God's creative word but a reflection that lacks the identity between word and thing ("let there be light and there was light"). Instead of being identical, human words give a knowledge of things, that is, human language always recognizes the difference between itself and things. If it did not know this difference, human language would be, like God's word, divinely and absolutely creative. To put this another way, God *makes* things knowable by making them exist. In contrast, things are named by humans in order to have knowledge of what has been made.

Benjamin makes clear that the object of this theory of language, while deeply related to a religious context, is not "biblical interpretation nor subjection of the Bible to objective consideration as revealed truth" (*SW* 1, 67). What is at stake for Benjamin in his account of God's word is to show that language is an "ultimate reality, perceptible only in its manifestation" (*SW* 1, 67). Even the word of God is subject to this account since God is also what makes language perceptible in its manifestation (again, as in the phrase "let there be light"). If God is associated with revelation, and man with reason, then what Benjamin is arguing can be summarized exactly in a phrase he quotes from Hamaan, a late eighteenth-century German theologian and philosopher: "*Language, the mother of* reason and *revelation,* its alpha and omega" (*SW* 1, 67). If language is the mother of revelation and reason, God and human, then it is the beginning and end of all that can exist. The fundamental task of language is then to communicate this state. But what this also means in terms of Benjamin's theory is that language always communicates something other than itself even when it appears to communicate only itself. This claim, which lies at the center of Benjamin's understanding of human language, is his solution to the problem announced at the beginning of this essay. However, instead of favoring one side or another of this problem (whether language is about itself or about things external to it), Benjamin argues that it is both. By communicating itself, human language indicates how external things exist within language: it is their linguistic being that occurs in language. In this way, language is both about itself and what is external to it. This understanding asserts that human knowledge, since it is based on the human act of naming, cannot be confused with whatever thing or object is known. A lamp is both a lamp and a name, and that is why it can exist as an object and also why we have knowledge about it.

Suggested further reading

Peter Fenves. *Arresting Language.* Stanford: Stanford University Press, 2001. 199–226.

Rodolphe Gasché. "Saturnine Vision and the Question of Difference: Reflections on Walter Benjamin's Theory of Language." In *Benjamin's Ground.* Ed. Rainer Nägele. Detroit: Wayne State University Press, 1988. 83–104.

"On the Program of the Coming Philosophy" (1918)

> Experience is the uniform and continuous multiplicity of knowledge.

Already in 1913, Benjamin had asked "what then does experience signify?" ("Experience," *SW* 1, 3). This early essay, a critique of how adult experience is divorced from spirit, introduces a concept that will become increasingly complex in the course of Benjamin's critical writing. "On the Program of the Coming Philosophy" is a first example of this complexity. Here, experience is no longer viewed as a source of intergenerational conflict. Rather, as this essay's title indicates, the concept of experience is taken up as the central question to be examined in modern philosophy if it is to resolve the issue that stands in the way of its future development. By resolving this issue, Benjamin is also taking up a question that, he asserts, remains unsolved within Kant's philosophy: the relation of knowledge to experience, or, to put this in the temporal terms Benjamin uses, the relation between something lasting and something ephemeral. Traditionally, what is lasting has always been preferred over what is ephemeral whenever knowledge is at stake. The result of this preference is that philosophy has pursued knowledge as something independent from the fleeting nature of experience. In this essay, Benjamin seeks to establish that experience is in fact "the immediate, if not the only object of . . . knowledge" (*SW* 1, 101) and that such experience is central to the future development of philosophy. However, what Benjamin presents in this essay is by no means the example of such a philosophy. Benjamin will only outline a "program of research" (*SW* 1, 106). The emphatic anticipatory character of this essay has the effect of postponing any confirmation of what Benjamin says into the future – a tendency that will return in later and more politically oriented writings. As a result, the essay is both a diagnostic and a prognostic exercise. By diagnosing what is wrong with the past (its failure to develop fully a concept of experience for philosophy), Benjamin identifies the task that the future needs to undertake (to develop such a concept). Pursuing this task is not, however, an outright rejection of the past. Despite the limitation of Kant's understanding of experience, Benjamin insists that the approaching philosophy must find its place in Kant's systematic thought.

Benjamin's emphasis on Kant reflects the important presence of this philosopher in the philosophical teaching of German universities at this time. Especially important in this regard were the neo-Kantians – also known as the Marburg School. Benjamin's account of experience, however, differs from the one that prevailed in this school. Benjamin charges that the neo-Kantians neglected to pay attention to a necessary element of experience, its continuity.

Failure to recognize this element leads to a relation between experience and knowledge in which the former is always regarded as inferior since it was viewed as a series of separate events that could only yield a fragmentary knowledge. In effect, such experience was nothing more than consciousness of the world.

For Benjamin, this view of experience was essentially the world view of the Enlightenment. Against this view, Benjamin seeks to elaborate "a higher concept of experience" (*SW* 1, 102). At the same time, Benjamin seeks to preserve the essential core of the Kantian system despite its inability to develop this higher concept. The Kantian influence on his thinking here is evident as he considers "which elements of the Kantian philosophy should be adopted and cultivated, which should be reworked, and which should be rejected" (*SW* 1, 102). But, as Benjamin's subsequent remarks make clear, the one thing he will not reject in Kant is the systematic aspect of his thought. By preserving this aspect, Benjamin reveals at this stage of his intellectual development a strong tendency for "systematic unity or truth" (*SW* 1, 100). Despite Benjamin's recognition that fulfilling this tendency requires a struggle, he does not yet relate the necessity of this struggle to any doubt about the value or attainability of systematic unity in general. In this respect, Benjamin still operates within distinct metaphysical intentions, as his characterization of experience in the following phrase indicates: "this future metaphysics, this higher experience" (*SW* 1, 102).

After laying out what future philosophy must do, Benjamin turns to this concept of "higher experience." Instead of defining it positively, he describes first what it is not. He brands Kant's version of experience as being essentially a "mythology" based on "the notion ... of an individual living ego which receives sensations by means of its senses and forms its ideas on the basis of them" (*SW* 1, 103). He then goes on to state that this is no different from "primitive peoples ... who identify themselves with sacred animals and plants and name themselves after them" (*SW* 1, 103). What such primitive peoples do is nothing less than "empirical consciousness" for Benjamin, that is, it is experience reduced to mere observation of the world by a subject. Against this, Benjamin elaborates what he calls "epistemological (transcendent) consciousness." He states that this consciousness is only valid "under condition that it be stripped of everything subjective" (*SW* 1, 104). Here, Benjamin's claim on behalf of a consciousness that is not subjective is a claim for an experience that can then take its place beside knowledge as something no longer defined according to one person.

What is at stake, for Benjamin, in this concept of consciousness is the relation of "all of experience immediately to the concept of God, through ideas" (*SW* 1, 105). Benjamin defines this further when he states that the task of future philosophy is "the discovery or creation of that concept of knowledge which . . . makes not only mechanical experience but also religious experience logically possible" (*SW* 1, 105). What Benjamin aims at is an account of knowledge which, even though derived from "higher experience," will encompass both this higher experience and the lower experience that remains primarily empirical. By setting such a goal for future philosophy, Benjamin's concept of experience emerges as inherently metaphysical to the extent that it directs itself towards a systematic and unified account of all experience. Such an account, however, is by no means attainable or confirmable at this stage. All Benjamin can offer by way of strengthening this claim is the necessity expressed in the following sentence: "A way must be found in metaphysics to form a pure continuum of experience; indeed, it seems that the true meaning of experience is to be found in this area" (*SW* 1, 106).

In an attempt to lay out a path that will confirm this necessity as actual truth, Benjamin asserts that this confirmation can be attained if knowledge is related to language:

> the great transformation and correction which must be performed upon the concept of experience . . . can be attained only by relating knowledge to language . . . [and] . . . a concept of knowledge gained from reflection on the linguistic nature of knowledge will create a corresponding concept of experience which will also encompass realms Kant failed to truly systematize. The realm of religion should be mentioned as the foremost of these.   (*SW* 1, 108)

This task of relating knowledge to language will return, notably in the preface to his *Origin of the German Tragic Drama*, but with different consequences. Gone will be the confidence in metaphysics as the future of philosophy, or, to put this more strongly into its context, metaphysics will no longer promise a future in which the significance of the modern world is to be found. But what will not disappear is the sense of something continuously present.

As Benjamin recognizes at the end of this essay, experience cannot rise to the claims he makes for its place in philosophy unless it possesses some continuous element that will offset its ephemeral, temporal existence. Benjamin finds this element in what he calls the doctrinal or teaching character of experience (the word Benjamin uses is *Lehre*, which can refer to doctrine and the teachings of an individual religion or philosophy). This claim on behalf of experience is based on a unity of experience that is more than just a sum of different experiences. Without this unity, Benjamin argues, there is nothing to teach, only a collection of different experiences. Yet, when Benjamin tries to provide a positive account of this unity of experience, he is forced to equate it with the source of existence without explaining how or why this is so. In the end, the essay only offers this: "there is a unity of experience that can by no means be understood as a sum of experiences, to which the concept of knowledge as teaching is *immediately* related in its continuous development" (*SW* 1, 109). With this sentence, the evidence for the unity of experience claimed by Benjamin becomes a negative knowledge; it relies upon what experience cannot be understood as. We can know what this experience is different from but not what it is. Complicating things further is the question of how teaching, in "its continuous development," is "immediately related" to this unity. To pursue this question is to identify precisely what Benjamin is struggling with here: a relation that only metaphysics could imagine as a necessary goal. The goal here, as Benjamin gives voice to it, is "something absolute," but how this absolute is to be experienced is left unresolved. The essay displaces into the future what it cannot affirm, here and now.

Suggested further reading

Howard Caygill. "The Program of the Coming Philosophy." In his *Walter Benjamin: The Color of Experience.* London: Routledge, 1998. 26–29.

(b) Raising criticism 1919–1925

Benjamin completes five significant works between 1919 and 1925. Uncommonly, all five appear in print not just during his lifetime but within one to two years of being written. Except for the "Critique of Violence," these works represent Benjamin's most sustained study of literature and literary language from a philosophical viewpoint. They are also the product of a period in which Benjamin tries to shape his thinking and writing towards the academic career that, in the end, never materializes. Not only does he feel at odds with the formal requirements of academic writing but his approach to literature, inflected through a theory of language as well as his philosophical and historical interests, sets his writing apart from what was expected within literary study in the university.

The first and last of the works presented in this section are written for a specific academic goal. The study of the concept of criticism in the German Romantics is Benjamin's first dissertation, completed at the University of Berne in 1919. This work proves to be Benjamin's only academic success. Facing incomprehension, Benjamin is forced to withdraw his second dissertation, *Origin of the German Tragic Drama,* from consideration at the University of Frankfurt in 1925. This disparity between Benjamin's critical thinking and the expectations of the university subsequently proves decisive for his career as writer and critic. After this failure, Benjamin relinquishes all pretense to satisfying academic demands in his writing.

The first dissertation, published as a book in 1920, is a study of the theory of literature developed within early German Romanticism by a group collectively known as the Iena Romantics. Specifically, it is an account of the concept of criticism that accompanied this theory. The important step taken by this theory – and this is what attracts Benjamin to the subject – is that criticism is given, for the first time, a role as a serious and philosophically engaged activity. This dissertation marks Benjamin's first sustained attempt to move the task of criticism away from commentary and establish its relevance in relation to problems that have defined the development of both philosophy and history.

Between these two dissertations, three other significant essays are written in this period: "Critique of Violence," "Goethe's *Elective Affinities*," and "The Task of the Translator." Of these three, the first is the only essay not to address literature and language as its principal subject. The "Critique of Violence" is one of Benjamin's most topical essays. Not only does its focus on violence and law, and the nature of the proletarian general strike, register the occurrence of such strikes in Switzerland in 1918 and Bavaria in 1919, but the subject matter also suggests the political interest that gains fuller voice in his later Marxist-influenced writings. Despite such a leaning, this essay does remain methodologically closer to his intellectual concerns in this period – especially the idea of "pure means" advanced in this essay as well as his embedding of the idea of criticism within a historical and philosophical context.

The essay "Goethe's *Elective Affinities*" is both a detailed study of Goethe's novel and a critical attack on the aesthetics of the George School, in particular the mythical role of the poet cultivated by this School. As in the 1919 dissertation, the significance of literature is located in the individual work rather than the external conditions in which it is produced. A consequence of this emphasis is that the task of criticism is oriented towards philosophy and the nature of language. This philosophical and linguistic aspect is developed in "The Task of the Translator," an essay whose title proves misleading for those seeking practical guidance in the craft and practice of translation. Benjamin's focus is on the significance of translation in general, that is, he is concerned with the significance of the fact that such a thing as translation occurs as well as what this occurrence says about literature and language.

The second dissertation, on German Baroque drama, published as a book in 1927, further defines what Benjamin has been working toward in his analyses of the Iena Romantics and Goethe. In many ways this book is the culmination of the first part of his career. Both intensely theoretical – the preface is infamous for its difficulty – and historically detailed concerning the literary works he interprets, the *Origin of the German Tragic Drama* provides an account of a genre and a period in German literature that has received scant attention in Benjamin's time or before. His interpretation places this drama at the threshold of modernity and does so by using a critical method that accesses the historical significance of this genre through its form – a method that will have considerable influence on figures in the Frankfurt School (and most notably Adorno who is the first to offer a university seminar devoted to this book).

The Concept of Criticism in German Romanticism (1919, pub. 1920)

We all still live very deeply immersed in the discoveries of Romanticism.

This work is the first serious attempt in the twentieth century to come to terms with the significance of a group of essayists, critics, and poets known as the Iena Romantics. Based in Iena between 1798 and 1804, this group had a powerful effect on how the activity of criticism came to be understood within modernity. In their hands, criticism passed from judging whether a literary work was good or bad to becoming the means through which the significance of literature and art in general could be articulated.[1] In the hands of the Iena Romantics, criticism became the means of giving literature and art a significance that was no longer merely aesthetic. Rather, they understood artistic work as a medium in which all other forms of knowledge could be reflected. By this means, criticism and its object, art, made a claim to philosophical seriousness. Benjamin examines this claim by focusing on two of the principal figures active in this group, Friedrich Schlegel and Novalis. However, *The Concept of Criticism in German Romanticism* is not just a study of their writings. It also situates German Romanticism within its philosophical roots.

Foremost among these roots is the work of the German Idealist philosopher Johann G. Fichte, who provided the Romantics with the idea of a "reflexive thinking." What "reflexive" means here is that the subject and the means by which that subject recognizes itself are one and the same. Benjamin has also explored this kind of relation in his essay "On Language in General" when he defines language as both a means of communication and what is communicated by that means, that is, it is both immediate and mediating. In his study of the Romantics, Benjamin places this idea at the origin of their theory of art. The task of their criticism was to produce this idea as the essential property of art, in short, as the universal idea of art. What is unique about this task, for Benjamin, is its difference from "the modern concept which sees criticism as a negative court of judgment" (*SW* 1, 152). In contrast, the Romantic concept is completely positive.

The reason for Benjamin's attraction to this concept of criticism appears in an abstract he prepared for the dissertation. In it, he refers to "today's depraved and directionless practice of criticism."[2] The sense that criticism has lost its significance is what leads Benjamin to a historical recovery of the Iena Romantics. This is not to say that Benjamin's own critical position can be aligned with the Romantics – *The Concept of Criticism* provides ample evidence that he is aware of the limitations of their position. Rather, Benjamin's interest in the Iena Romantics' concept of criticism lies in the relation of this concept to what he calls a "historical-problematic" at the very beginning of *The Concept of Criticism*, that is, a problematic that recurs in the history of criticism. For Benjamin, the Romantic theory of art and criticism is an important step in the history of this problematic because of the seriousness with which it offers a solution by redefining the task of criticism.

Benjamin's analysis of this solution focuses on the systematic tendencies of the Romantics (especially their attempt to make literature a medium of infinite interconnectedness for philosophy, science, etc.). According to these tendencies, the task of criticism is to dissolve the individual work into the universal medium to which all art belongs. In Benjamin's words: "criticism is therefore the medium in which the restriction of the individual work refers methodically to the infinitude of art and finally is transformed into that infinitude" (*SW* 1, 152). As Benjamin states here, criticism is the medium that allows art to become universal. Consequently, a truly critical work is also a work of art. Here, the reflexive principle derived from Fichte finds its artistic fulfillment: criticism is both a means of recognizing the idea of art and the realization of that idea. Art thus finds its consummation in an absolutely reflexive relation between itself and its criticism. To paraphrase one of Schlegel's aphorisms, also cited by Benjamin, the criticism that reveals the idea of art in poetry must also be a poem. As a result, the idea of art thereby "suspend[s] the difference between criticism and poetry" (*SW* 1, 153). The consequences of this claim should not be glossed over too quickly. What the Romantics are claiming is the following: if a poem needs criticism in order to realize its relation to the idea of art, then every individual work of art is incomplete because of this need. But if such a criticism must also be a poem, then criticism is incomplete with respect to the idea of art. What the Romantics express here is an absolute theory of art based on the incompleteness or individuality of every work of art. The reflexive thinking at the heart of this claim is clear: art is absolute in its inability to be absolute. The task of the Romantic concept of criticism is to reveal and reflect this absolute in every work, itself included.

Benjamin recognizes that the theory of art and criticism advanced by the Iena Romantics marks a "decisive overcoming of aesthetic dogmatism" (*SW* 1, 154), that is, of a tendency to subject all aesthetic matters to external rules or expectations. In this respect, Benjamin adds, the Romantics "secured a basic concept that could not have been previously introduced into the theory [of art] with any definiteness: the concept of the work" (*SW* 1, 155). Consequently, *The Concept of Criticism* recovers the decisive role the Iena Romantics played in defining the significance of the work of art according to "an immanent structure specific to the work itself" (*SW* 1, 155). In other words, works of art are not reducible to a rule they are supposed to reflect or represent; they are individuals and independent of any such external definition.

Examining a work immanently is of the utmost importance for Benjamin – as his analysis of the university in "The Life of Students" and of Hölderlin's poetry in "Two Poems by Friedrich Hölderlin" already confirm. Still, despite the fact that the Iena Romantics are a decisive factor in introducing an immanent approach to the work of art into modern criticism, their attempt to justify the individuality required by this approach remains unsatisfactory for Benjamin: "the cardinal principle of critical activity since the Romantic movement – that is, the judgment of works by immanent criteria – was attained on the basis of Romantic theories which in their pure form certainly would not completely satisfy any contemporary thinker" (*SW* 1, 155). Benjamin then goes on to criticize the Romantics in the following terms: "In order to express the individuality of this unity of art, Schlegel strains his concepts and grasps at a paradox. Otherwise the project of expressing the highest universality as individuality was not to be consummated" (*SW* 1, 166–67). Yet, as if to make clear where his interest lies, Benjamin concludes: "Schlegel simply gave a false interpretation to a valuable and valid motive" (*SW* 1, 167). The motive in question is Schlegel's attempt to prevent his theory of art from being misunderstood as nothing more than "an abstraction from empirical artworks." The issue Benjamin raises here is how to account for the significance of art without resorting to abstractions that deny the individuality of every work of art. For Benjamin, the weakness of the Romantics' position is that their attempt to avoid abstraction left them with nothing more to grasp than the assertion of a paradox: the universal is the individual. As a result, the question of what forms the specific individuality of a work of art remains unresolved.

Benjamin's criticisms of the Iena Romantics unveil an issue central to the modern practice of criticism: how to account for the significance of art without resorting to its merely aesthetic properties. Later, in his essay on Goethe's *Elective Affinities*, this significance will be named the "truth-content" of art. But here, Benjamin still uses the vocabulary of the Romantics, who expressed such content as the "prosaic element" in art. Despite the Romantic claim, again paradoxical, that prose is the idea of poetry, it is evident that their emphasis on the prosaic represents an important development for Benjamin. This becomes even clearer when he introduces the notion of the "sobriety of art" expressed by Friedrich Hölderlin, a poet from this period, and links it to the prosaic:

> the thesis that establishes [Hölderlin's] philosophical relation to the Romantics is the principle of the sobriety of art. This principle is the essentially quite new and still incalculably influential leading idea of the romantic philosophy of art; what is perhaps the greatest epoch in the West's philosophy of art is distinguished by this basic notion . . . the prosaic is a familiar metaphorical designation of the sober.   (*SW* 1, 175)

The importance Benjamin assigns to this principle cannot be underestimated. Sobriety and the prosaic stand in contrast to a history that attached ecstatic, manic qualities to art – as if art were the outpouring of some possessed or magical state. To Benjamin, Hölderlin's notion of sobriety clarifies what the Romantics were aiming at. This sober view states that artworks "are essentially neither appearances of beauty nor manifestations of immediately inspired emotion" (*SW* 1, 177) – to cite the two approaches to art that dominate prior to the Romantics. Instead, with this shift to the prosaic, the understanding of art takes a decisive modern turn. Benjamin emphasizes this modern aspect when he draws attention to the basic principles of the theory of art present "in so eminently conscious a master as Flaubert" and adds that they can also be found in the Iena Romantics (*SW* 1, 177).

By emphasizing this sober understanding of art in his study of the Iena Romantics, Benjamin also draws attention to the central task confronted by their writings on art: the legitimation of criticism. This task aims at uncovering the sober, prosaic nature of art. The goal of such a criticism does not pretend to serve "as an objective court of judgment on all poetic production" (*SW* 1, 178). Instead, the goal of criticism is the recognition of art in general; in other words, criticism finds its legitimation as the theory of art. The Romantics located this legitimation in the interchangeability of all art and criticism. However, Benjamin notes, this theory of art remained, in the last analysis, something "less demonstrated than postulated" (*SW* 1, 174). While this remark again distinguishes Benjamin's position from the Iena Romantics, the question remains: after marking his differences with the Romantics, precisely what is at stake for Benjamin in *The Concept of Criticism*?

In a letter written one month after completing his dissertation, Benjamin declares, "I have written an esoteric Afterword for the dissertation, it is for those to whom I would have to present it as *my* work" (*GB* 1, 210). The Afterword to *The Concept of Criticism* examines the relation between Goethe's concept of criticism and that of the Iena Romantics. Between these two, Benjamin states, lies "the pure problem of criticism" (*SW* 1, 178). This is a "pure" problem because, in Benjamin's analysis, the way these two accounts relate to one another forms the basic problem of any philosophy of art. Benjamin's study is content to pose the question occasioned by this relation, that is, his interest lies in the identification of a question that neither Goethe nor the Romantics could resolve. As Benjamin observes: "The Romantics did not resolve, or even pose, this question, any more than Goethe did. They all work together to introduce this question to the history of problems. Only systematic thought can resolve it" (*SW* 1, 183). Where Goethe left unresolved the question of form in relation to art, the Iena Romantics left unresolved the question of the content of art. It is the resolution of the Goethean and the Romantics' position that Benjamin leaves for systematic thought. What is at stake in this resolution is the question of what content the form of art can possess. Rather than repeating the paradoxes the Romantics offered in response to this question, Benjamin's study seeks to clarify the task they were unable to fulfill: the task of legitimating a meaningful content for criticism and thus also for art. In this context, the significance of Benjamin's *The Concept of Criticism* has less to do with providing an answer to the question of what kind of content is appropriate to criticism than with establishing the question of just such a content as the task of modern criticism. In doing so, Benjamin's account of the Iena Romantics not only shows the extent to which they were distinct from what the literary-historical label "Romantic" has come to mean but also shows the extent to which this dissertation becomes the setting for articulating the critical questions with which his subsequent writings engage.

Suggested further reading

David Ferris. "Benjamin's Esoteric History of Romanticism," *Studies in Romanticism* 31.4 (1992), 455–80.

Rodolphe Gasché. "The Sober Absolute: On Benjamin and the Early Romantics." In David Ferris, *Walter Benjamin: Theoretical Questions*. Stanford: Stanford University Press, 1996. 50–74.

John McCole. "The Immanent Critique of Romanticism." In McCole, *Walter Benjamin and the Antinomies of Tradition*. Ithaca, NY: Cornell University Press, 1993. 71–114.

Samuel Weber, "Criticism Underway: Walter Benjamin's *Romantic Concept of Criticism*." In *Romantic Revolutions*. Ed. Kenneth Johnston *et al.* Bloomington: Indiana University Press, 1990. 302–19.

"Critique of Violence" (1921)

> The ultimate insolubility of all legal problems.

The essay "Critique of Violence," written between *The Concept of Criticism* and his essay on Goethe's *Elective Affinities*, engages a very different subject matter from the one developed in *The Concept of Criticism*. Dealing with the place of violence within the state and its legal foundation, this essay is more clearly concerned with political issues than anything else Benjamin writes at this time. Yet, as the essay's title conveys, a concern with criticism is at stake, in particular, the possibility of a position from which violence or force (the German word *Gewalt* means both) can be subject to criticism.

The first sentence of this essay clearly sets out the task of criticism: to show the relation of violence to law and justice. Here, critique is understood not as judgment but as a means of obtaining an understanding of law and justice. Benjamin's analysis begins by giving two accounts of violence. The first of these is called natural law. According to natural law, violence occurs as something humans cannot avoid (in the sense that violence is something humans are naturally disposed to). As a result, its significance can only be judged according to the end it produces. The second account is called positive law. This law rejects the use of an end as a means of justifying violence. Instead, it regards violence as "a product of history." Accordingly, the question of whether violence is justified falls upon the particular set of historical circumstances that lead to violence (in the sense that violence is not the result of a natural disposition but the result of a specific historical situation).

These two accounts of law indicate the existence of two mutually exclusive principles. Natural law judges the legality of violence by reference to the end sought (this is the "end justifies the means" argument). In contrast, positive law only judges the legality of the means, that is, whether violence, the means, is justified by the specific historical situation that produced it. According to this approach, if the historical circumstances justify violence, then the end is also justified.

Benjamin presents these two mutually exclusive positions in order to develop another position. The methodological move adopted here recalls the afterword to *The Concept of Criticism* when Goethe and Iena Romantics appear as two sides of a single problem. In the "Critique of Violence" there is also a single problem. Benjamin opens this problem up by observing that positive law, unlike natural law, must evaluate violence (decide whether it is sanctioned or not by its historical circumstances). The "Critique of Violence" is by and large the tracing of the consequences of this distinction.

Benjamin develops these consequences by asking "what is the meaning of this distinction?" (*SW* 1, 237–38). Benjamin's initial response to the question he poses is to turn again, as he had done in *The Concept of Criticism*, to a "philosophico-historical view." As he remarks towards the end of this essay, only such a view "makes possible a critical, discriminating, decisive approach" (*SW* 1, 251). With this approach, Benjamin aims at the discovery of "a standpoint outside positive legal philosophy but also outside natural law" (*SW* 1, 238). From this standpoint, the critique of violence emerges.

The analysis of this standpoint first focuses on the way in which a legal system attempts to control violence. The reason why a legal system attempts this control is because violence can undermine that same system. Since law controls violence, what is at stake in this attempt is not one legal end or another but rather the legal system itself. Benjamin observes: "violence, when not in the hands of the law, threatens it not by the ends that it may pursue but its mere existence outside the law" (*SW* 1, 239). Why this violence is so threatening to the law is not simply because it is external. It can also threaten the law from the inside. Benjamin notes that this is most evident when the law appears to control violence by sanctioning its use. The example of such a use cited by Benjamin occurs in the right of workers to strike.

Benjamin remarks that the strike is the only form of violence that the state allows a legal subject to perform. When the right to strike is understood as a use of force for certain ends, it becomes a form of violence whose purpose is to extort a certain response from an employer. In this case, it is no longer a simple "severing of relations" since it makes demands in order to counter a violence (working conditions, salary, etc.) "exercised indirectly by the employer"

(*SW* 1, 239). For both the workers and the state, what is present here is the right to use violence or force to attain certain ends. Because this right is shared by both, the legal system is not threatened by such a strike. However, the case of a general strike differs for Benjamin.

The general strike is seen by the state as an abuse of the right it has permitted workers to exercise. Faced with such a strike, the state is forced to recognize that its own principle (the right to use violence for an end) can be used against itself. What the state views with "indifference" in a regular strike is now viewed as harmful to its interests and its existence. Benjamin refers to the position the state now finds itself in as an "objective contradiction" – objective because the state has put itself in this situation and has done so not because of a contradiction in the law but because of its desire to preserve the rule of law (in this aspect the state acts in an entirely consistent manner despite being forced to respond in contradictory ways).

In his interpretation of this situation, Benjamin remarks that "in a strike the state fears above all else that function of violence which it is the object of this study to identify as the only secure foundation of its critique" (*SW* 1, 240). The function that is so threatening and which comes to the fore in the general strike is the ability of violence "to found and modify legal conditions." This function is defined as the law-making aspect of violence. This aspect stands in direct contrast to the way in which the state uses violence to preserve its law. The contradiction Benjamin wishes to bring out here focuses on the state's double use of violence. Benjamin asserts, "all violence is either law-making nor law-preserving" (*SW* 1, 243). What this contradiction allows Benjamin to get at is "the problematic nature of law itself" (*SW* 1, 243). This problematic nature can be summarized as follows: the violence used by the state to preserve its laws is also the violence that overturns those laws by establishing other laws.

The problem Benjamin focuses on becomes clearer in the relation of the state to capital punishment. Such punishment is an example of how law uses violence. However, in claiming jurisdiction over life and death, what is at stake is not a sentence that suits a crime but upholding the right of the law to exercise this violence in order to preserve itself. To make his point, Benjamin cites the example of primitive legal systems in which the death penalty is imposed for crimes against property. This disproportionate use of the death penalty reveals that the crime is less important than the establishment of law. For Benjamin, the violence of this disproportion indicates "something rotten in the law" (*SW* 1, 242). Above all else, what is rotten is that the law has no other justification in this case than its self-preservation when faced with a crime which threatens to establish the lawfulness of that crime precisely because it has gone unpunished.

In this example, where the law decides cases of life and death, its violence takes on the character of fate; as Benjamin puts it, "violence crowned by fate is the origin of law" (*SW* 1, 242). What preserves law is its ability to act as though it were fate.

What emerges from Benjamin's treatment of capital punishment is that the "secure foundation" for a critique of violence comes from the exercise of violence itself, that is, a critique is not imposed from the outside. Although Benjamin already speaks of such a critique as "a standpoint outside positive legal philosophy but also outside natural law" (cited above), there is no contradiction here. The standpoint that exists outside positive and natural law is one that has nothing to do with the orientation toward an end that characterizes these two kinds of law. In contrast, the standpoint Benjamin articulates here emphasizes means divorced from ends since his focus concentrates on the means used by law. When he draws attention to the contradictory use to which the law puts this means, Benjamin moves towards an understanding of what he calls "pure means." Why he calls this "pure means" is because, in a contradictory use of means, it is impossible to decide what end is being pursued. As a result, the effect present in "pure means" is neither law-making nor law-preserving – these are merely two functions violence serves.

The difficulty involved in establishing pure means as a standpoint that is neither law-making nor law-preserving surfaces when Benjamin poses the following question:

> How would it be . . . if all the violence imposed by fate, using justified means, were in irreconcilable conflict with just ends, and if, at the same time, a different kind of violence arose that certainly could be either the justified or unjustified means to those ends but was not related to them as means but in some different way?   (*SW* 1, 247)

This question envisages a violence other than the one understood by legal theory. But this other violence is also present in and through the violence at work in the law. This is where the difficulty and the unresolved question of this essay occurs. The violence Benjamin calls "pure means" must relate to the law in a way that has nothing to do with ends (this is what is meant by the phrase "not related to them as means," that is, not related to them as the means of achieving an end but as pure means).

The "different way" in which this relation occurs remains a question, yet its significance is immense. Benjamin explains: it "would throw light on the curious and at first discouraging discovery of the ultimate insolubility of all legal problems" (*SW* 1, 247). This last remark points to "pure means" as something that the law cannot control. Accordingly, the law also registers the presence of a violence it cannot submit to an end or a purpose, that is, cannot subject to the operation of law. How this violence relates to the law is the problem this essay poses. As Benjamin shows in this essay's subsequent analysis of unmediated violence in myth, further distinctions are necessary if a pure means of violence is not to end up being once again complicit with the violence of ends practiced by the law. The task of destroying this complicity, Benjamin concludes, "poses again, ultimately, the question of pure unmediated violence" (*SW* 1, 249). To answer this question is to establish the critical standpoint from which this task may be carried out.

Benjamin offers a philosophico-historical approach to this question: "the critique of violence is the critique of its history . . . a gaze directed only at what is close at hand can at most perceive a dialectical rising and falling in the law-making and law-preserving forms of violence" (*SW* 1, 251). Consequently, the critical standpoint of this essay is derived from a philosophical account of history. Here, his reflections on criticism in *The Concept of Criticism* show their close affinity with his thinking on violence. In that earlier work, Benjamin's interest lay in the historical unfolding of a single problem. In the "Critique of Violence," Benjamin analyzes law in relation to the problem posed throughout its history by this notion of a "pure means" whose non-violence escapes a legal system that can only operate through its ability to mediate violence (means understood as only a means to an end). It is from the law putting itself in contradiction with itself that Benjamin posits a problem at the very foundation of the law itself. By naming this problem "pure means," a means without ends, Benjamin also poses the question of how such a means exists – a question that is even more difficult to resolve since it is posed within the realm of politics. If the question of a "politics of pure means" must remain open in this essay, that is, remain a question, Benjamin nonetheless offers an analogy for it: "there is a sphere of human agreement that is non-violent to the extent that it is wholly inaccessible to violence: the proper sphere of 'understanding,' language" (*SW* 1, 245). By asserting that language is a "pure means," Benjamin is calling upon language as a means that knows neither right nor wrong. As such a means, language exists without regard to the ends to which it may be put. Yet, in the end, Benjamin will "only point to pure means in politics as analogous to those which govern peaceful intercourse between private persons" (*SW* 1, 245), that is, analogous to language.

The critical standpoint this essay leaves us with is thus dependent on an analogy between politics and history on the one hand, and language on the other. To a large extent, this analogy establishes the critical project that will define the course of Benjamin's thinking in these years: unfolding the historical significance of the critical force present in language. This project emerges as

Benjamin shifts from "pure means" in the "Critique of Violence" and takes up the question of appearance and the "expressionless" in his study of Goethe's novel *The Elective Affinities*.

Suggested further reading

Alex Düttman. "The Violence of Destruction." In *Walter Benjamin: Theoretical Questions*. Ed. David Ferris. Stanford: Stanford University Press, 1996. 165–84.

Werner Hamacher. "Afformative, Strike: Benjamin's 'Critique of Violence.'" In *Walter Benjamin's Philosophy: Destruction and Experience*. Ed. Andrew Benjamin. Manchester: Clinamen Press, 2000. 108–35.

Beatrice Hanssen. *Critique of Violence: Between Poststructuralism and Critical Theory*. London: Routledge, 2000. Introduction and chapter 1.

Tom McCall. "Momentary Violence." In *Walter Benjamin: Theoretical Questions*. Ed. David Ferris. Stanford: Stanford University Press, 1996. 185–206.

"Goethe's *Elective Affinities*" (1919–1922, pub. 1924–1925)

> Only the expressionless completes the work.

Written between 1919 and 1922, this essay forms a bridge between the completion of the first dissertation on the Romantics and the beginning of his second dissertation devoted to the origins of the German *Trauerspiel* or mourning play. Despite its title, this long essay focuses not just on Goethe's novel *The Elective Affinities*, but also on the interpretation of Goethe published in 1916 by Friedrich Gundolf, a member of the George Circle who was then the foremost literary critic in Germany. Benjamin's treatment of Gundolf is uncompromising, and reflects a view he had long held. Already in a fragment from 1917 he had written: "Gundolf has nothing convincing to say about Goethe" and "his book is a veritable falsification of knowledge" (*SW* 1, 98, 99). But, despite this harsh criticism, Benjamin is not simply dismissive. Instead, he relates Gundolf's work to a consequence of his theory of language, namely, "language itself must contain the possibility of enabling such a book to contest its own semblance" (*SW* 1, 99). The emphasis Benjamin places on language as a critical reference point in this 1917 fragment not only confirms the importance of his 1916 essay on language but anticipates the role language plays as the primary analogy for the critical function he gives to "pure means" in the "Critique of Violence."

Given the context of Benjamin's other writings in this period, it is not surprising to find that the task of criticism again receives prominence in this essay. At the outset, Benjamin distinguishes strongly between critique and "commentary" and then goes on to state: "critique seeks the truth content of a work of art; commentary its material content" (*SW* 1, 297). Yet, there is no simple choice between these two aspects of the work of art. For Benjamin, their relation is determined by "that basic law of literature according to which the more significant the work, the more inconspicuously and intimately its truth content is bound up with its material content" (*SW* 1, 297). With this law, Benjamin does not simply present a theory of literature but also reflects on the possibility of interpreting the truth of a particular work of art.

This theory of literature emerges as Benjamin describes the historical dimension of works of art: "the works that prove enduring are precisely those whose truth is most deeply sunken in their material content" (*SW* 1, 297). To endure, truth is sheltered in the material aspect of a work. However, history does not reveal this truth. As the work of art endures, "the concrete realities [of the work] rise up before the eyes of the beholder all the more distinctly the more they die out in the world" (*SW* 1, 297). With this rising up, the material content comes to the fore and, since it is this content that the later critic must confront, the first task of interpretation is commentary. In Benjamin's view, the production of commentary not only is part of the history of works of art but is also the way in which they "prepare for their critique" (*SW* 1, 298). Thus, the purpose of history is to preserve the truth content of a work of art so that critique may eventually bring out this content.

Benjamin's promise of a truth content requires a word of caution lest this be understood as the revelation of some hidden meaning. What is at stake for Benjamin is not something hidden. This becomes clear when the term "the expressionless," around which Benjamin organizes his analysis, is considered. This term also deserves caution since what Benjamin refers to is not something ineffable and beyond understanding. Rather, the expressionless is very much grounded in the existence of a work, and above all else in its means of expression, its language.

The third part of this essay develops the meaning of the expressionless. The word appears in the course of an analysis that defines art's relation to philosophy. This analysis begins by stating "critique ultimately shows in the work of art the virtual possibility of formulating the work's truth content as the highest philosophical problem" (*SW* 1, 334). By aiming at a virtual possibility, critique however stops short of formulating such a problem. Accordingly, critique of the work of art can only show the appearance of what Benjamin calls here – and had also done so in *The Concept of Criticism* – the "ideal

of the problem" (*SW* 1, 334). Where philosophy is concerned with the existence of such an ideal problem, critique must remain within the realm of
appearances.

Benjamin defines this ideal of the problem in the following terms. First, he
states: if an answer provides a solution to all philosophical problems, then,
this answer cannot be obtained by questioning. Why this is so is because the
question leading to the answer must also be considered part of the answer.
In other words, the answer is still part of the problem it is trying to resolve.
According to this logic, every answer is determined by the question from
which it arises. Therefore, to the extent that a philosophical problem poses
a question, it is already entrapped by its method of inquiry. This situation,
in which a question or problem cannot be divorced from the answer each
already presumes, leads Benjamin to conclude: "It follows that there is no
question which . . . encompasses the unity of philosophy. The concept of this
non-existent question seeking the unity of philosophy by inquiry functions
in philosophy as the ideal of the problem" (*SW* 1, 334). In this concept of a
question that cannot exist, the problem of providing a unity for philosophy is
given an ideal form, that is, a form that has no actual existence.

Although art expresses this problem, its manner of expression is not philosophical; rather it belongs to appearance. Benjamin observes, "in every true
work of art an appearance of the ideal of the problem can be discovered" (*SW*
1, 334). For critique to discover this problem in a work of art is to discover the
truth content of that work. In this case, the task of criticism is to show how a
work of art presents this problem – and to do so without becoming philosophy.
What is then at stake for Benjamin is an account of what art is in difference
from its sibling, philosophy.

Given the critical issues Benjamin brings to the fore in this essay, it is not
surprising that his analysis of Goethe's *Elective Affinities* seeks to view "the effect
of the novel as the expression of an inherent problematic" (*SW* 1, 339). After
stating this, Benjamin goes on to say that "only an incorruptible rationality,
under whose protection the heart might abandon itself to the prodigious,
magical beauty of this work, is able to cope with it [the problematic]" (*SW* 1,
339). In this incorruptible rationality, the sobriety of Hölderlin emphasized in
The Concept of Criticism appears – and Benjamin will again refer to Hölderlin
in his account of the expressionless in the work of art.

This soberness refuses the temptation to lose one's heart or succumb completely to magical beauty in the work of art. Despite the rationality of Benjamin's
approach, he does not reject the role or place of such seductions in a work
of art. In fact, they are necessary elements in any work. However, the danger
Benjamin perceives is that when they are used to account for the unity of a

work of art, their effect is to "petrify" it or make it appear "as if spellbound in a single moment" (*SW* 1, 340). It is precisely this effect that the expressionless interrupts. The way in which Benjamin develops this interruption recalls the significance of a violence no longer defined by ends from the "Critique of Violence" essay. Benjamin writes:

> The expressionless is the critical violence which, while unable to separate appearance from essence in art, prevents them from combining. It possesses this violence as a moral dictum. In the expressionless, the sublime violence of the true appears as that which determines the language of the real world according to laws of the moral world. For it shatters whatever still survives as the legacy of chaos in all beautiful appearance: the false, errant totality – the absolute totality.   (*SW* 1, 340)

What is moral is the refusal to accept the confusion of appearance and essence. In this case, the expressionless is neither appearance nor essence but rather a violence that prevents their co-existence in an artwork from joining to become a totality. As such, it is not a destructive or negative element since its role is only to prevent them from combining with one another.

Benjamin's preservation of appearance and essence exhibits the tightrope he is walking between the traditional terms used to define art and the reconfiguration of these terms through the expressionless. What this reconfiguration aims at is described in the following, highly metaphorical description:

> the expressionless compels the trembling harmony to stop and through its objection immortalizes its quivering. In this immortalization the beautiful must vindicate itself, but now it appears to be interrupted precisely in its vindication, and thus it has the eternity of its content precisely because of that objection.   (*SW* 1, 340)

The interruption performed by the expressionless results in a rethinking of the role of beauty in the work of art. Through the objection maintained by the expressionless, the beautiful becomes what it is, an appearance, that is, its content is restricted to its appearance. This happens because the expressionless arrests the movement by which the beautiful seeks to vindicate itself by projecting its aesthetic charms as the essence of art.

The target of the critique mounted through the expressionless is the dominant role that "beautiful appearance" has played in the understanding of art under the influence of Schiller. In contrast to this tradition, Benjamin puts forward a theory of art that places interruption at its center. While this position suggests a movement from unity and totality on the one hand, and towards incompletion on the other, that is not the full picture.

Benjamin speaks of interruption as something that completes the work: "Only the expressionless completes the work, by shattering it into a thing of shards, into a fragment of the true world, into the torso of a symbol" (*SW* 1, 340). What completes the work is also what fractures it. The sense of a work as a fragment, so central to the Iena Romantics, is strongly present here. Also present is Hölderlin's understanding of the caesura, the break that forcefully interrupts a line of poetry. After referring to Hölderlin, Benjamin writes: "that caesura, in which, along with harmony, every expression simultaneously ceases in order to give free reign to an expressionless power inside all artistic media" (*SW* 1, 341). What is important about this example of the expressionless is the way it is used to name a content for art that has nothing to do with any source of significance external to an individual work. Here, Benjamin answers the question left suspended at the end of *The Concept of Criticism*: the expressionless, the caesura, is the content of art, its truth. Moreover, as Benjamin remarks, this truth cannot be ascribed in any way to the poet or author: "something beyond the poet interrupts the language of poetry" (*SW* 1, 351).

What is beyond the poet is marked by what Benjamin calls the "expressionless." The point at which the truth content of the work of art is discovered is then at the limit of what appears or can be expressed in such a work. This theory turns the traditional concept of beautiful appearance on its head. Instead of this appearance being understood as representing some absent essence, this representation, by being interrupted, leads to a reinterpretation of what essence means in relation to the beautiful – and accordingly mounts an uncompromising critique of representation as providing access to the significance of art.

This critique of representation appears most forcefully when Benjamin explains how the beautiful operates as a veil that no longer works to conceal something behind it. Instead of lifting the veil to see what is hidden by appearance, Benjamin states that the beautiful is only in its true form when it is seen as appearance. As a result, any attempt to unveil this appearance and reveal what is behind the veil is to misunderstand the significance of beauty and appearance in art. Its purpose is not to be unveiled or, as Benjamin states: "the task of art criticism is not to lift the veil but rather, through the most precise knowledge of it as a veil, to raise itself for the first time to the true view of the beautiful" (*SW* 1, 351). In this respect, criticism's task is to complete the work of art. However, in distinction to the Iena Romantics, who privileged criticism over and above art (and thereby turned art into a form of criticism), Benjamin attempts to locate this completion in a content that belongs to art – which the Romantics failed to do. For Benjamin only the expressionless answers to the truth of this content but, since it is without expression, and since, like the caesura, it is an interruption, it has nothing to represent except its occurrence. In Benjamin's essay on Goethe's *Elective Affinities*, this occurrence defines a work as a work of art.

Suggested further reading

David Ferris. "Benjamin's Affinity: Goethe, the Romantics and the Pure Problem of Criticism." In *Walter Benjamin and Romanticism*. Ed. Andrew Benjamin and Beatrice Hanssen. London: Continuum, 2002. 180–96.
Sigrid Weigel. "The Artwork as Breach of Beyond: On the Dialectic of Divine and Human Order in Walter Benjamin's 'Goethe's *Elective Affinities*.'" In *Walter Benjamin and Romanticism*. Ed. Andrew Benjamin and Beatrice Hanssen. London: Continuum, 2002. 197–206.

"The Task of the Translator" (1921, pub. 1923)

> translation does not transmit subject matter.

This essay, originally published as the preface to Benjamin's translation of poems from Baudelaire's *Les fleurs du mal*, has achieved the status of a work that cannot be avoided in discussions of translation and its theory. Despite such a status, this essay is far from being a practical guide to translation. Rather it is concerned with the question of what significance translation possesses. Benjamin's response to this question is to show how translation attains its fullest meaning when we understand what its relation to language is. In this respect, the significance of translation is not restricted to simply providing another version of what a work represents.

From the very beginning, Benjamin takes away from translation the task of repeating in another language what an original work refers to through its language. Translation does precisely the opposite according to Benjamin: "[a literary work] 'tells' very little to those who understand it. Its essential quality is neither communication nor information" (*SW* 1, 253). This statement indicates how little this essay's concern with translation can be divorced from an understanding of what a literary work is. Furthermore, since a literary work says very little in the way of information, then the question of what can be translated is no longer a simple case of conveying the same content in another language.

In contrast to a translation based on content, Benjamin states that "Translation is a form" (*SW* 1, 254). Translation is a form for Benjamin because its significance is not decided by what the original work means. Benjamin explains this by reference to the German and French words for bread: "In the words *Brot* and *pain*, what is meant is the same, but the way of indicating it is not" (*SW* 1, 257). Form is the way of intending meaning, but, as the words *Brot* and *pain* indicate, each form by which bread is known belongs to a specific set of relations in each language. Because it is the task of translation to bring out these relations, translation is intimately related to how language is structured, and to how it means. Accordingly, the theory of translation is simultaneously a theory of language.

The relation of translation to the nature of language had already been hinted at in Benjamin's 1916 essay on language when he writes, "It is necessary to found the concept of translation at the deepest level of linguistic theory" (*SW* 1, 69). The proximity of translation to the nature of art had also been noted in *The Concept of Criticism* (*SW* 1, 154). The importance of the Romantics in establishing translation as more than a secondary activity recurs in this essay too. Accordingly, "The Task of the Translator" is not an isolated work within Benjamin's thinking between 1916 and 1921. Rather, it is the deepening of an already existing concern with language and the work of art.

The theory of language presented in this essay addresses the foreignness of languages. Previously, Benjamin had considered this foreignness in a more limited way (see "On Language as Such" [*SW* 1, 63] and the preceding section 3(a) on this essay). Now, the difference between a name and an object is thought across the multiplicity of languages. While translation offers an understanding of this difference, it is also for Benjamin a way of understanding a foreignness that belongs to all languages. Although this coming to terms remains a "temporary and provisional solution" because a "final solution" is "out of the reach of mankind," it still points the way to what Benjamin calls the "hitherto inaccessible realm of reconciliation and fulfillment of languages" (*SW* 1, 257). This realm is characterized as "pure language" in this essay and, like "pure means" and "the expressionless," it has a constitutive role to play even if its existence can only be inferred from translation.

Central to Benjamin's theory of language in this essay is his account of intention. Benjamin defines intention in language as the way in which language expresses meaning. According to this definition, a word can only intend a meaning or an object while maintaining its difference from that object. As something that intends, a word promises a meaning but cannot itself be what it means (or intends). This difference between a word and what it means indicates a deficiency that the historical development of languages continually strives to make up for or supplement. Benjamin describes this striving as something that not only occurs within an individual language but also occurs between languages because of the kinship of all languages with one another. Benjamin explains:

> kinship between languages consists in this: in every one of them as a whole, one and the same thing is meant. Yet, this one thing is achievable not by any single language but only by the totality of their intentions supplementing one another: the pure language.   (*SW* 1, 257)

Every single language is incomplete in some way, but in their multiplicity, languages relate to one another in such a way as to supplement one another. Benjamin locates this supplementing activity in intention (the way language means rather than what is meant). According to what Benjamin said earlier, this means that such an activity is located in the form of a translation. Because every language participates in this condition, Benjamin writes, "languages are not strangers to one another but are . . . interrelated in what they want to express" (*SW* 1, 255). As a result, the task of translation is to express this "innermost relationship of languages to one another" (*SW* 1, 257).

A direct consequence of this task is that translation "transplants the original into a more definitive linguistic realm" (*SW* 1, 258). The reason a more definitive realm appears is because the original possesses a relationship between its content and its language that is quite different from how these are related in a translation. Benjamin explains: "Whereas content and language form a certain unity in the original, like a fruit and its skin, the language of the translation envelops its content like a royal robe with ample folds. For translation signifies a more exalted language than its own and thus, compared to its own content, remains unsuited, overpowering, foreign" (*SW* 1, 258). By signifying a more exalted language, the meaning of a translation lies less in its own content than in the way it supplements the original work. By supplementing the original, translation signifies the pure language intended by both. This is why language always overpowers content in a translation.

While an original can be translated, Benjamin argues that a translation cannot be translated. The inability of a translation to be translated is not just a matter of redundancy. For Benjamin, it is what lies behind a key concept introduced early in the essay: translatability. He links the ability of a work to be translated to a "specific significance inherent in the original" (*SW* 1, 254). This is not, however, a specific meaning or object that the translation is to restate. Rather, it aims at a significance that makes translation possible in the first place.

Benjamin provides an account of this significance by comparing the relation between language and content in the original to the relation between a fruit and its skin. In the terms of this analogy, translation is possible because the skin (language) is unable to communicate what it gives a form to. Why this is so is because there would be no need for translation if language or the original work were able to communicate its content. This understanding is repeated when Benjamin writes: "In all language and linguistic creations, there remains in addition to what can be conveyed something that cannot be communicated" (*SW* 1, 261). Since language can only address "what is meant" by its "way of meaning" or its intention to convey that meaning, then all that can be translated by language is this intention. In other words, what every translation does is to convey in varying degrees a fundamental condition of language while remaining unable to dismiss that condition. In a closing remark, Benjamin points to this condition, distinguishing between the presence of form and content in different works:

> The lower the quality and distinction of [an original's] language, the
> greater the extent to which it is information, the less fertile a field it is
> for translation, until the utter preponderance of content, far from
> being the lever for a well-formed translation, renders it impossible.
> The higher the level of a work, the more it remains translatable even if
> its meaning is touched upon only fleetingly. This, of course, applies
> to originals only.   (*SW* 1, 262)

On the basis of its intentional form, its way of meaning, an original work establishes its translatability. This characteristic accords precisely with Benjamin's theory of language in this essay: translation, by supplementing the original, brings out the original work's relation to what is meant, relates to the work in the same way as one language relates to another. By undertaking this supplementary work, Benjamin asserts that the "tremendous and only capacity of translation" is "to regain pure language" (*SW* 1, 261). Here, translatability poses the question of what is meant by the language of the original work. For Benjamin translation can do this because, in the original, "what is meant is bound to the way of meaning of the individual word" (*SW* 1, 259–60). Through this aspect, the language of the original also belongs to pure language, that is, to a language which "no longer means or expresses anything but is, as expressionless and creative Word, what is meant in all languages" (*SW* 1, 261). If the original were such a pure language, translation could never exist because the original work would have no need to be supplemented by another language. Consequently, the purpose of translation is not to reveal this pure language in the original but rather to "allow [it] . . . to shine upon the original more fully" (*SW* 1, 260).

Since translation supplements an original for the same reason one language supplements another, no single translation is capable of realizing this pure language. Just as translation was "a temporary and provisional solution to the foreignness [of languages]" (*SW* 1, 257), so, here too, it is an equally provisional solution to the question posed by the intention of the original work. This provisional status accounts for why there can be more than one translation of a work as well as why translation is an index to the historical afterlife of an original work. Each historical context will supplement the original in a different way, that is, each historical context will express the original's relation to meaning precisely because language does not and cannot decide this relation. This inability is what preserves the language of the original as a language that translation can never complete. We may say bread and the French may say *pain*, but in doing so we have not answered what the French mean by this word but have merely repeated the intention present in each language, the intention to mean from which Benjamin draws a purity of language.

Suggested further reading

Andrew Benjamin. "The Absolute as Translatability: Working through Walter Benjamin on Language." In his *Philosophy's Literature*. Manchester: Clinamen Press, 2001. 105–22.

Carol Jacobs. "The Monstrosity of Translation." In her *In the Language of Walter Benjamin*. Baltimore: Johns Hopkins University Press, 1999. 75–90.

Paul de Man. " 'Conclusions': Walter Benjamin's 'The Task of the Translator.' " In his *The Resistance to Theory*. Minneapolis: University of Minnesota Press, 1987. 73–105.

Origin of the German Tragic Drama (1924–1925, pub. 1928)

> What I have written consists almost entirely of quotations. It is the craziest mosaic technique you can imagine.

Properly speaking, this is Benjamin's only book of criticism. Although his first dissertation on the Iena Romantics is published in book form, it lacks the sense of concentration and critical argumentation displayed here. Written between May 1924 and April 1925, this work was undertaken in order to secure a university teaching position. Its failure to accomplish this goal has become one of the legendary, if not defining, events of Benjamin's life. When the work was received with incomprehension at the University of Frankfurt, Benjamin had no other option but to withdraw it from consideration. Despite this summary judgment, the *Origin of the German Tragic Drama* became one of the most important critical works of the twentieth century. The importance of this work, however, lies not in Benjamin's treatment of its subject, Baroque drama, but rather in its account of modernity and ruin as well as its reinterpretation of allegory.

Although less true now than at that time, German Baroque drama was a forgotten and ignored form within literary study during the early decades of the twentieth century. Even Benjamin's turn to this genre will appear surprising in the context of the interests and issues explored by his principal writings between 1916 and 1924. However, the questions posed by this drama had attracted Benjamin. In two short unpublished texts from 1916, there occurs a first reflection on this form, properly known as *Trauerspiel* or mourning play.[3] Already, in this early writing, many of the central points of the later book emerge: the non-unified nature of the mourning play, how it relates to historical rather than mythic time, its emphasis on repetition, signified and signifier, its allegorical presentation of events and the relation of this mode of presentation to history. Benjamin's return to this genre is thus a return to an interest that predates *The Concept of Criticism*, the essay on Goethe, and his essay on violence. However, it is a return influenced by the problems and issues developed in those writings. In a letter written in March 1924, Benjamin makes clear that this book on the Baroque mourning play is related to the questions he pursued in his account of the Iena Romantics. Several references in the *Origin of the German Tragic Drama* clarify this relation further. For instance, in the third part of this book, Benjamin, after calling Romanticism an important correction to the Classicism that preceded it, goes on to assert that the Baroque "offers a more concrete, more authoritative and more permanent version of that correction" (*OGT*, 176). The correction is more permanent because it is not just a correction that belongs to a period in art, but, Benjamin claims, a correction to art itself.

The period that defines the historical context of the drama studied in this book is named for a style of expression that originated in Italy around 1600 before spreading to the rest of Europe. Baroque style is known for its elaborateness, profusion of detail, and extravagance. The style arose to dominance in the seventeenth century before falling into disfavor in the eighteenth century. Of the German authors who wrote Baroque drama, only two are remembered with any consistency in literary histories discussing this period: Andreas Gryphius (1616–64) and Daniel Caspar von Lohenstein (1635–83). Benjamin's book recovers the work of both Gryphius and Lohenstein but also of lesser-known authors such as Johann Christian Hallmann (1585–1647) and August Adolf von Hugewitz (1645–1706).

Benjamin presents the *Origin of the German Tragic Drama* in three parts. The first, called the "Epistemo-Critical Prologue," affirms Benjamin's reputation as a dense, complex, and difficult thinker, and it is the part that has received the most attention in the critical reception of this work. Except for the last section which speaks of these plays in general terms, the Prologue attempts no detailed analysis of the German mourning plays. Instead, its emphasis is on methodological questions.

Method, Benjamin states, is not just a "didactic mechanism"; rather, it possesses "a certain esoteric quality" (*OGT*, 27). This esoteric quality is located in a specific form of writing: the essay or treatise. For Benjamin, such a quality is present in the essay because it does not aim at the conclusiveness expected from a doctrine. The difference between the two, Benjamin continues, lies in their intentions: doctrine has a didactic purpose whereas the essay has an educational intention. The latter intention is the one he will pursue in his writing. Its method, Benjamin asserts, is what he calls the "authoritative quotation" (*OGT*, 28).

This definition of method in the essay prepares the main discussion of the mourning plays which occurs through extensive quotations. This method allows for a more digressive style of presentation in which interruption is emphasized over the kind of "uninterrupted progress of an intention" that characterizes didactic writing. Benjamin describes this interruptive method as follows: "Tirelessly thought begins from new things, returning in a roundabout way to the same object. This continual pausing for breath is the mode most proper to the process of contemplation" (*OGT*, 28). To cite Benjamin's image, this digressive method presents a mosaic composed of fragments, individual pieces of glass whose "value is all the greater the less direct their relationship to the underlying idea" (*OGT*, 29). As in the essay on Goethe's *Elective Affinities*, the truth content Benjamin aims at cannot be revealed directly; there is no fixed historical moment proper to its revelation. Accordingly, the method of presentation becomes the way in which the content of Benjamin's own writing is grasped.

The reason Benjamin adopts such a method is related to a distinction he makes between the use of method in knowledge and truth. Knowledge uses method as a means of acquiring whatever object it focuses on. As such, method is little more than a device enabling the possession of an object – even to the extent of creating this object in our consciousness. He argues that such a possession of knowledge results in the exclusion of any prior existence for an object since it has only been understood within consciousness. In contrast to this, Benjamin claims that an object has a prior existence "as something presenting itself." What this means is that the truth of an object resides in its presentation, its form, rather than in the content imposed on it by consciousness. For Benjamin, content must exist in the form or manner of presentation that belongs to an individual work.

To explain how and where this truth is to be experienced, Benjamin offers the following guidance:

> This content, however, does not come into view by being exposed; rather it is revealed in a process which might be described metaphorically as the bursting into flames of the husk as it enters the realm of ideas, that is to say an incineration of the work in which its form achieves the high point of its illuminating power.   (*OGT*, 31)

Many of the issues Benjamin emphasizes in the *Origin of the German Tragic Drama* are present in this sentence: the truth content does not endure; its manner of revelation leads to its destruction so that what remains is no more than a ruin; this truth content is only graspable as it enters the realm of ideas, that is, it is only graspable through what causes its destruction; this destruction realizes the significance of a work's form. From these characteristics, it is evident that Benjamin is not concerned with a fixed truth, an external reference point that can be called on over and over again throughout history. Since the destruction emphasizes the form of the work, and since the form only attains its greatest illumination at the most extreme point of its existence (its incineration), then, form is the decisive way in which content becomes present.

For Benjamin, this form is recognized as a "constellation," a word that will reappear in his later and more historically materialist thinking in the 1930s. Benjamin writes: "ideas are to objects as constellations are to the stars" (*OGT*, 34). What this means is that constellations do not tell us what individual stars are. All the same, constellations relate stars to one another in a way that gives them a form – a form that the stars play no role in determining since they cannot see how we see them. With this analogy, Benjamin draws attention to what is essential for him: ideas do not determine the content of stars, they only determine the relation of stars to one another. To confuse content and relation is to possess knowledge in all the bad senses that possessing conveys. On the other hand, to distinguish relation is to allow a truth to appear that expresses no intention to possess. Because the constellation has no intention to possess the stars (as if recognizing a group of stars told us anything about what stars are), they are not changed; they remain what they were before the constellation is recognized.

Benjamin's concept of a constellation does two things. First, it preserves the individual existence of each star (thereby refusing any intention to possess them according to some external idea). Second, it rescues these stars from an insignificant, arbitrary relation to one another but does so without resorting to the traditional relation between form and idea whereby the form that an arrangement of stars possesses is understood as having been derived from the idea it represents. The idea imposes its understanding on the stars through such a notion of form. However, because what is imposed cannot possibly be true (that is why it is imposed), recognition of its falseness opens the door for other ideas to be put in its place. These other ideas all possess what Benjamin calls intention, that is, they indicate a truth that is imposed on one form or another so that those forms are understood as the expression of that intention. But, because they are imposed, they do not express the truth of those forms. Since truth should not be something that is imposed, it must therefore occur in a different relation of idea and form, a relation in which neither idea nor form seeks to determine the other. Instead, and this is where Benjamin's thinking differs from the Platonic context in which these words are so often discussed, the idea is understood to emerge from the constellation as the truth of the arrangement it presents. What is important and different here is that truth does not occur in either the form or the idea but in this different relation of idea to form. And this is why, to cite a famous phrase from this Prologue, "truth is the death of intention" (*OGT*, 36). Intention, which belongs to the didactic whenever form is defined by a pre-existing idea, has no place in such a relation; truth is its interruption.

One important consequence of this understanding of truth is that the ideas present in it all have a finite, individual existence within a specific form. Again, an analogy used by Benjamin provides an explanation: "Every idea is a sun and is related to other ideas just as suns are related to each other" (*OGT*, 37). In this image, ideas are related to one another in a form that emphasizes their difference from one another. In the sentence following the one just cited, Benjamin refers to these ideas or suns as essences and then defines their truth as what they present through their relation one with another: "The harmonious relationship between such essences is what constitutes truth. Its oft-cited multiplicity is finite; for discontinuity is a characteristic of the 'essences . . . which lead a life that differs utterly from that of objects and their conditions'" (*OGT*, 37). Each idea has a finite existence. Consequently, each idea is discontinuous with another idea just as the suns in different solar systems are discontinuous with one another. When Benjamin refers to the relation of these suns as truth, he also places a discontinuity at the center of truth. Here, what Benjamin says about the essay, its interruptions and pauses for breath, should be recalled. In these discontinuities, truth is present but it is a truth that allows nothing to be deduced from it since its discontinuity contains the interruption of knowledge rather than an intention to masquerade as knowledge. It is this interruption, in the form of allegory, that Benjamin explores in the mourning play.

With all the emphasis on truth and truth content in the introduction to the *Origin of the German Tragic Drama*, one might expect that the second and third sections of this book present a non-historical understanding. This is discounted early in the second section, when Benjamin defines the "artistic core" of the mourning play: "historical life, as it was conceived at that time, is its content, its true object. In this it is different from tragedy. For the object of the latter is not history, but myth" (*OGT*, 62). With this distinction between the mourning play as history and tragedy as myth, Benjamin rescues the Baroque play from the genre it has frequently been confused with. At the same time, the emphasis on historical life does not mean that these plays are simply a representation of the history of their time. Instead, Benjamin's argument is that these plays, by including the events of their time, present history as something subject to the form of art. This argument points to how these plays claim history as their content. They appropriate the events of their time and put them in relation to one another in a way that only art can do. Here, the artifice Benjamin emphasizes in these plays becomes significant. The artifice of these plays interrupts the relation between the historical events they present and the world these events are drawn from. As a result, historical events are strewn across these plays as ruins that cannot be put together again in any coherent representation of the past. By emphasizing this aspect, the critical task Benjamin undertakes in this book is to rescue the mourning play by establishing the significant role it plays in the formation of a modern understanding of history and art in terms of ruins.

Central to this rescue is Benjamin's reinterpretation of allegory. His rethinking of the relation of form and idea and his refusal to see one as merely a derivative representation of the other (in a doctrinal or didactic way) provide the basis for this reinterpretation. Benjamin quickly dispenses with the conventional view that allegory is nothing more than "an illustrative image and its abstract meaning" (*OGT*, 162). For Benjamin, this medieval view is displaced in the Baroque by a "modern allegorical way of looking at things"

(*OGT*, 162). The illustrative aspect of allegory gives way to discontinuity and fragmentation: "In the field of allegorical intuition, the image is a fragment, a rune . . . the false appearance of totality is extinguished" (*OGT*, 176). Not only does the image remain a fragment but, as Benjamin notes, there is such a profusion of allegorical images at work in the mourning plays that their effect is one of constant artifice. It is through their artifice, their "extravagant pomp," that these dramas proclaim, for Benjamin, "a deep rooted intuition of the problematic character of art" (*OGT*, 176). The historical significance of the Baroque mourning play resides in this intuition.

This problematic character appears when art renounces an external and eternal source of meaning – precisely the move made in the theoretical introduction to this book in the relation of form to idea. Where such a source is historical (in the sense that an intention controlling art's development through time is asserted), the purpose of art is to affirm that history. In the mourning play, Benjamin changes both this understanding of history and art's relation to such a history. Instead of representing history, these plays present the experience of what history is:

> When, as is the case in the mourning play, history becomes part of the setting, it does so as writing. The word "history" stands written on the countenance of nature in the characters of transience. The allegorical physiognomy of nature-history, which is put on stage in the mourning play, is actually present in the form of the ruin. In the ruin, history has physically merged into the setting. And in this guise, history does not assume the form of the process of an eternal life so much as that of irresistible decay . . . Allegories are, in the realm of thoughts, what ruins are in the realm of things. This explains the baroque cult of the ruin. (*OGT*, 177–78)

In allegory, art inhabits the ruin that history is. History, in the sense Benjamin understands here, occurs in a writing that makes no claim beyond its fragmentary images, that is, its allegorical images. This perception demands not only that history be seen as such images but, like the stars in the night sky, that these images can be arranged in a constellation. Such an arrangement, however, is transient. What appears in the art of the Baroque drama brings this transience to the fore in an allegorical account of history.

As Benjamin observes in the introduction to this book, origin is an "entirely historical category" (*OGT*, 45). Why this is so is because an origin is "what is restored and reestablished," that is, it is something produced by subsequent history as an explanation of why certain events occurred. In this respect, origin holds to the definition of allegory Benjamin provides towards the end of the

Origin of the German Tragic Drama, namely, allegory "means precisely the non-existence of what it represents" (*OGT*, 233). For Benjamin, the Baroque mourning play originates in this modern account of allegory. But what is also at stake here is the form that history receives from this allegorical presentation. History is no longer a content to be represented by art. Instead it is presented in the "structure and detail" of the artwork. This shift in the origin of historical significance is the decisive contribution of this work. Benjamin rescues this sense from the Baroque by interpreting "the extraordinary detail of [its] allegorical references" (*OGT*, 182). His interpretation proceeds in a way that allows the historical meaning of art to appear.

To bring out this meaning, Benjamin has to rescue the Baroque mourning play from both itself and its critical reception. The plays have to be rescued from themselves because, as Benjamin observes, "From the very beginning [these plays] are set up for that critical decline which befell them in the course of time" (*OGT*, 181). As a form whose allegorical nature was content to settle "in consciously constructed ruins" (*OGT*, 182), they offered no interest to a criticism that expressed the symbolic and the beautiful as the content of art. Still less did this criticism attempt to open the question of history as it is presented in art. Not only did Benjamin do this but he did it in a way that, by seeking "to make historical content . . . into philosophical truth," sought to provide "the basis of every important work of art" (*OGT*, 182).

From a form of drama marginalized within literary history, Benjamin offers a crucial recognition of what defines the modern sense of art as a work, but does so by demonstrating the close affinity of form with historical meaning. To achieve this, as the theoretical introduction points out, is to demand a transformation in how criticism understands the content of art. At this point in the development of Benjamin's thinking, allegory fulfills that demand.

Suggested further reading

Christine Buci-Glucksmann. *Baroque Reason: The Aesthetics of Modernity*. London: Sage Publications, 1994.

Peter Fenves. "Tragedy and Prophecy in Benjamin's *Origin of the German Mourning Play*." In his *Arresting Language: From Leibniz to Benjamin*. Stanford: Stanford University Press, 2001. 227–48.

Max Pensky. *Melancholy Dialectics*. Amherst: University of Massachusetts Press, 1993.

Samuel Weber. "Genealogy of Modernity: History, Myth and Allegory in Benjamin's *Origin of the German Mourning Play*," *Modern Language Notes* 106.3 (1991), 465–500.

(c) Culture, politics, and criticism 1926–1931

With the completion of the *Origin of the German Tragic Drama*, Benjamin marks the conclusion of what he will later call his "German cycle" (*C*, 322). The ending of one cycle and the beginning of another, however, occurs with some overlap. Before completing his study of the mourning play, Benjamin had already begun a very different kind of writing. No longer discursive in overall design, nor academic in intention, this writing took the form of what he called *Denkbilder* or "thought-images." *One-Way Street*, written between 1923 and 1926 but not published until 1928, is the work that first registers this different style of thought. Although many of Benjamin's other writings between these years are less experimental in format, they still reflect the significant change in the orientation of his thinking that appears in *One-Way Street*.

This change arises directly from his introduction to Marxism. This occurs during his stay on Capri in 1923 when he reads Lukács for the first time. This new interest develops further under the influence of Asja Lacis, a Latvian Bolshevist, also visiting Capri, and with whom Benjamin became enamored. His interest in Lacis led him to visit Moscow from December to February 1926–27, providing him with direct experience of a communist political state. With the increasing influence of left-wing politics on his thought, it is not surprising that Benjamin flirted with the idea of joining the Communist Party although, unlike his brother Georg, he did not make this commitment. For Benjamin, the appeal of communism lay in its vitality as a force of action. In this respect, he distinguished communism from other political movements that tended to define themselves according to goals. This disavowal of a goal is crucial to Benjamin who, in 1926, states bluntly: "there are no meaningfully *political* goals" (*C*, 301). If the political cannot be understood in terms of goals, then its significance becomes a matter of the historical forces at work in the present. Given this context, the change reflected in Benjamin's thinking during this period can be seen as the beginning of his attempt to shape a criticism capable of facing the historical and political significance of contemporary experience. The overbearing presence of a history and a politics such as the one shaped by German fascism – a movement that overwhelmingly understood its significance in terms of goals – made such an account increasingly imperative.

Benjamin's writings from this period exhibit a breadth of interests that is hardly imaginable from the more literary focus of his writings between 1916 and 1926. There are essays on hashish; a group of writings from 1927 dealing with Russia and his visit to Moscow, most notably his *Moscow Diary*. He also writes on pornography and the state, Chaplin, gambling, the destructive character, the cultural history of toys, graphology; there are radio broadcasts on the Lisbon earthquake, the Firth of Tay railway disaster, a Kafka story. In addition he produces reviews of fiction such as Alfred Döblin's *Berlin Alexanderplatz*, reviews of critical and historical writings, as well as writings on contemporaries such as Bertolt Brecht, Julien Green, Robert Walser, and other still living authors such as André Gide and Paul Valéry. From these varied writings, this chapter will focus on those that form the core of his critical thinking in these years: *One-Way Street*, "Surrealism," "On the Image of Proust," "Theories of German Fascism," and "Karl Kraus."

One-Way Street (1923–1926, pub. 1928)

> To grasp topicality as the reverse of the eternal in history.

The epigraph Benjamin invents for *One-Way Street* defines the influence that led to its writing while pointing to where this street should be located: "This street is named / Asja Lacis Street / after her who / as an engineer / cut it through the author" (*SW* 1, 444). "Cutting through" can be rendered a little more literally as a "breaking through," which also has all the character of a breakthrough in Benjamin's thought. In this respect, the title of this book is important: in a one-way street there is no turning back. However, Benjamin is not making an absolute break with his past. Looking back in 1928, he writes that in *One-Way Street* "an earlier aspect of my character intersects with a more recent one" (*C*, 293). This sense of an intersection points to Benjamin's awareness that this new direction, while radically different from the style and method of his earlier writings, does not turn away from the concerns of those writings. Rather, Benjamin develops the more theoretical and philosophical concerns of his earlier writing through materials that test these concerns in a more historical and political way. A remark from this time summarizes the position Benjamin now adopts: "any definitive insight into theory is precisely dependent on practice" (*C*, 248).

Benjamin also gives *One-Way Street* a specific historical and intellectual context. When Benjamin confesses that "the book owes a lot to Paris"

(*C*, 333), he means that it was there he "discovered the format for the notebook [*One-Way Street*]." Specifically, he is referring to the surrealist movement in Paris and one of its principal participants, Louis Aragon. While the format of *One-Way Street* has its origin in surrealism's exploration of the everyday, Benjamin's text lacks the dreamlike character that surrealism cultivated. Instead, he practices a writing that offers reflections on objects of everyday experience under titles such as "Filling Station," "Breakfast Room," "Gloves," "Toys," and "Mexican Embassy." There are also theses on writing and criticism – some of the latter presented in parallel columns underlining the dialectical mode of presentation that characterizes this work. There are records of dreams too, a visit to Goethe's house, recorded souvenirs of places traveled to, as well as more theoretical reflections.

Adorno aptly summarizes Benjamin's aphoristic style of writing as well as the montage-like format of this work in the following terms: "the fragments of *One-Way Street* . . . aim less to give a check to conceptual thinking than to shock through their enigmatic form and thereby set thinking into motion."[4] Adorno's use of the word shock – a word that will become increasingly important in Benjamin's thinking in the 1930s – characterizes the non-discursive character of this work. Yet, rather than import this later term prematurely, the montage format of *One-Way Street* can also be seen as extending to the point of rupture the digressive method described in the Prologue to the *Origin of the German Tragic Drama*. The discontinuous presentation of *One-Way Street* interferes with any easy assimilation of its sections according to an underlying idea. The political aspect of *One-Way Street* emerges here. The concept of an underlying, unifying idea is identified as a hallmark of bourgeois thinking – especially when it is used to justify the historical significance of such a class. In *One-Way Street*, Benjamin sets out to present experience in a way that is no longer subservient to the representation of such ideas.

As the titles of various sections in *One-Way Street* indicate, contemporary experience claims attention but without asserting any all-encompassing narrative that would frame the experience of the present within a history. The following entry from *One-Way Street* makes explicit that such a narrative has no hold on the present:

> *Torso.* – Only he who can view his own past as an abortion sprung from compulsion and need can use it to full advantage in every present. For what one has lived is at best comparable to a beautiful statue that has had all its limbs broken off in transit, and that now yields nothing but the precious block out of which the image of one's future must be hewn. (*SW* 1, 467)

In the passage of history (its transit), the past loses its signifying details. In this way, the past no longer dominates the present. If it did, the meaning of the present would only be the result of the past – in such a case the present and therefore our experience could have no meaning of its own. Since the past is interrupted like an abortion, this leaves the present as the time in which the future is shaped but, as Benjamin points out, this future is only created as an image. Since this image only exists in the present, the future to which it refers for its meaning does not yet exist. The image is in this sense a torso, a ruin that cannot be completed. This incompleteness confirms that the image can only belong to the present.

This emphasis on the image reflects Benjamin's growing interest in it as the primary means by which meaning and significance are expressed. Here, the word Benjamin uses to describe each of the small texts that make up *One-Way Street* becomes important. They are "thought-images" or *Denkbilder* (sometimes also translated as thought-figures). This term indicates not only the role that the image occupies in his thinking but also the extent to which knowledge (both historical and philosophical) occurs as a succession of images. With this alignment of experience and knowledge in the image, Benjamin not only transposes the concerns of his preceding writings on literature into a more general cultural critique, but also finds a way to account for the role of the critic in relation to contemporary experience.

The section entitled "This Space for Rent" takes up the question of criticism in the contemporary world. It opens with the pronouncement "Fools lament the decay of criticism" (*SW* 1, 476). What such fools fail to understand is that the world in which criticism was at home is no more. The kind of criticism rejected here is one that relies on a world in which "perspectives and prospects counted and where it was still possible to adopt a standpoint" (*SW* 1, 476). In such a world, perspective and standpoint represented what was real. To Benjamin, this kind of criticism is a "lie" or even just "sheer incompetence." When Benjamin explains why this is so, there appears an argument that will later provide the basis of his most well-known essay, "The Work of Art in the Age of Its Technical Reproducibility":

> Today the most real, mercantile gaze into the heart of things is the advertisement. It tears down the stage upon which contemplation moved, and all but hits us between the eyes with things as a car, growing to gigantic proportions, careens at us out of a film screen. And just as the film does not present furniture and facades in completed forms for critical inspection, their insistent, jerky nearness alone being sensational, the genuine advertisement hurls things at us with the tempo of a good film. Thereby "matter-of-factness" is finally dispatched. (*SW* 1, 476)

In a world where images repeatedly "hit us between the eyes," a criticism based on standpoint has no significant role since it can find no place in which to establish itself. Equally, "matter-of-factness" no longer holds its sway over understanding because the distance necessary to this point of view has been torn down. Already, the critique of distance that characterizes Benjamin's later analyses of photography and film can be discerned here.

Although the contemporary experience of word and image (in the advertisement) renders obsolete a criticism based on distance and contemplation, this is not to say that the task of criticism has been relinquished by Benjamin. The section entitled "The Critic's Technique in Thirteen Theses" considers its survival even as it admits that the critic is now a "strategist in the literary struggle" (*SW* 1, 460). *One-Way Street* is an example of this strategic approach. Through the montage-like organization and the aphoristic quality of this work, Benjamin attempts to embody the present in such a way that its significance is experienced. This approach avoids a single standpoint and, in doing so, asserts that such a standpoint is no longer a means to comprehend contemporary experience. As the strategic character of this critical writing emerges, the vocabulary that has dominated his preceding writing (poetized, expressionless, unpresentable, idea and ideal, etc.) disappears.

Suggested further reading

Margaret Cohen. "Benjamin Reading the *Rencontre*." In her *Profane Illumination: Walter Benjamin and the Paris of the Surrealist Revolution*. Berkeley: University of California Press, 1993. 173–92.
Michael Jennings. "Walter Benjamin and the European Avant-Garde." In *The Cambridge Companion to Walter Benjamin*. Ed. David S. Ferris. Cambridge: Cambridge University Press, 2004. 18–34.
Henry Sussman. "Walter, the Critic." In his *The Task of the Critic*. New York: Fordham University Press, 2005. 75–98.

"Surrealism. The Last Snapshot of the European Intelligentsia" (1929)

> A dialectical optic that perceives the everyday as impenetrable, the impenetrable as everyday.

As Benjamin observes, surrealism is the first movement to put forward a radical concept of freedom since the writings of the nineteenth-century anarchist Mikhail Bakunin. In this essay, Benjamin examines how surrealism sought to relate this concept of freedom to contemporary experience in a revolutionary way. His analysis of these tendencies is largely diagnostic; it seeks to draw conclusions about the relation of freedom to politics within the experience offered by surrealism. While Benjamin sympathizes with the revolutionary claims of this movement he also remains aware of its shortcomings:

> There is always, in such movements, a moment when the original tension of the secret society must either explode in a matter-of-fact, profane struggle for power and domination, or decay as a public demonstration and be transformed. At present, Surrealism is in this phase of transformation.   (*SW* 2, 208)

For Benjamin, surrealism has fallen into decay despite its early promise to integrate all facets of experience in an absolute way, so absolute in fact that, for surrealism, there appeared to be no distinction between waking and sleeping, consciousness and the unconscious. Yet, in its emphasis on these terms, surrealism expresses its central concern with experience and this is precisely the aspect that influenced Benjamin's writing and conception of *One-Way Street*.

In his analysis of the surrealist movement, Benjamin coins a phrase that offers a summary of the direction of his thinking in these years: *profane illumination*. This phrase is coined as Benjamin traces surrealism's tendency to celebrate intoxication as its contribution to a history of revolt against Catholicism – undertaken by writers such as Rimbaud, Lautréamont, and Apollinaire. Benjamin writes: "the true, creative overcoming of religious illumination certainly does not lie in narcotics. It resides in a profane illumination, a materialistic, anthropological inspiration, to which hashish, opium, or whatever else can give an introductory lesson" (*SW* 2, 209). Characteristic of Benjamin's thinking here is that the shortcomings of a movement should become a positive force since once sifted through the lens of critical analysis they provide an "introductory lesson." The critical method he employs here is dialectical: surrealism's deficiencies express the problem that points to what it could not achieve, that is, the true, creative overcoming that resides in profane illumination.

According to Benjamin, the precise nature of surrealism's weakness lies in its recourse to a trick: "the trick by which this world of things is mastered – it is more proper to speak of a trick than a method – consists in the substitution of a political for a historical view of the past" (*SW* 2, 210). The weakness lies in a substitution. Surrealism does not in this respect alter the past, it merely replaces one view with another. Yet, despite their recourse to this trick, Benjamin acknowledges that the surrealists "are the first to liquidate the sclerotic liberal-moral-humanistic ideal of freedom" (*SW* 2, 215). This acknowledgment reveals the question guiding Benjamin's analysis: once this ideal of freedom is liquidated, on what foundation can a revolutionary politics be developed without falling back again into the ideologies of the past?

Intoxication – which Benjamin also experimented with (see "On Hashish") – is linked by the surrealists to revolutionary experience. But, as Benjamin points out, the effect of their intoxication is "to subordinate the methodical and disciplinary preparation for revolution entirely to a praxis oscillating between fitness exercises and celebration in advance." This praxis fails because surrealism could only produce "an inadequate, undialectical conception of the nature of intoxication" (*SW* 2, 215–16). Rather than using intoxication as a means of overcoming the distinction between such basic categories of experience as sleeping and waking, consciousness and the unconscious, Benjamin asserts that dialectical thinking must be given a central role if the political significance sought by surrealism is to be achieved. The failure of surrealism to produce a revolutionary politics leads Benjamin to pose – and answer – the following questions:

> Where are the conditions for revolution? In the changing of attitudes or of external circumstances? This is the cardinal question that determines the relation of politics to morality and cannot be glossed over. Surrealism has come ever closer to the Communist answer. And that means pessimism all along the line. Absolutely. Mistrust in the fate of literature, mistrust in the fate of freedom, mistrust in the fate of European humanity, but three times mistrust in all reconciliation: between classes, between nations, between individuals.   (*SW* 2, 216–17)

Mistrust and pessimism fuel the movement towards communism. Surrealism did move close to communism but not to the point where its revolutionary claims could avoid the pessimism and mistrust that fueled the communist answer. A principal concern of this essay is to avoid such pessimism. Characteristically for Benjamin, an answer will not be sought by simply advocating an alternative to surrealism. True to the immanent method of his earlier works, he begins an analysis that attempts to draw out of surrealism the revolutionary understanding it could not accomplish.

Benjamin develops his account of surrealism by turning to a text by one of its principal figures: Louis Aragon's *Treatise of Style*. Benjamin first notes Aragon's distinction between metaphor and image but then observes that this distinction yields a significance that has little to do with questions of style in writing:

Nowhere do these two – metaphor and image – collide so drastically and so irreconcilably as in politics. For to organize pessimism means nothing other than to expel moral metaphor from politics and to discover in the space of political action the one hundred percent image-space.

(*SW* 2, 217)

Benjamin clarifies that this turn to image and its space is a turn towards what "can no longer be measured by contemplation" (*SW* 2, 217). In *One-Way Street*, it was the advertisement that tore down "the stage upon which contemplation moved" (*SW* 1, 476). Now, what is found in place of that stage is the "image-space."

The aim of Benjamin's rejection of contemplation is to fulfill what he calls "the double task of the revolutionary intelligentsia," namely, "to overthrow the intellectual predominance of the bourgeoisie and to make contact with the proletarian masses" (*SW* 2, 217). What has prevented the completion of such a task is the failure of the intelligentsia to make such a contact. The persistence of a contemplative understanding of art and philosophy is cited as the reason for this failure: "the intelligentsia has failed almost entirely in the second part of this task because it can no longer be performed contemplatively." He then goes on to observe, "yet this has hindered scarcely anybody from approaching it again and again as if it could, and from calling for proletarian poets, thinkers, and artists" (*SW* 2, 217). To avoid such failure, another mode for poetry, thought, and art is required. Benjamin calls this other mode image-space and it is the task of the profane illumination first undertaken by the surrealists to initiate us into such a space. With such an initiation, there arises what Benjamin calls politics: the space born of the collision and irreconcilable difference between image and metaphor, action and contemplation. As the closing sentences of this essay indicate, Benjamin already sees technology as the means by which this image-space will become real in the body of the collective masses – a thesis that will find its fullest extension in "The Work of Art in the Age of Its Technical Reproducibility."

Suggested further reading

Margaret Cohen. *Profane Illumination: Walter Benjamin and the Paris of the Surrealist Revolution*. Berkeley: University of California Press, 1993.
Sigrid Weigel. "'Body- and Image-Space': Traces through Benjamin's Writings." In her *Body- and Image-Space: Rereading Walter Benjamin*. London: Routledge, 1996. 16–29.

"On the Image of Proust" (1929)

> After the self-satisfied inwardness of Romanticism, Proust came along.

In 1925–26, Benjamin had worked on the German translation of Proust's monumental seven-volume novel *A la recherche du temps perdu*. Unlike the preface to his translations of Baudelaire, this essay is not concerned with translation but with the significance of the image in Proust's writing – a focus that already underlines how much this account of Proust is, as Benjamin claims, a "companion piece" to the surrealism essay (*C*, 352). Despite this claim, Benjamin will only refer to surrealism once, yet when he does, he reveals how central surrealism is to his understanding of Proust:

> He lay on his bed racked with homesickness, homesick for the world distorted in the state of similarity, a world in which the true surrealist face of existence breaks through. To this world belongs what happens in Proust, as well as the deliberate and fastidious way in which it appears. It is never isolated, rhetorical, or visionary; carefully heralded and securely supported, it bears a fragile, precious reality: the image. (*SW* 2, 240)

In these sentences, three key terms of this essay appear: surrealism, similarity, and image. Although surrealism is not developed beyond this single reference, its influence is crucial, particularly when he insists on the relation of surrealism to a world "distorted in a state of similarity."

What Benjamin has in mind when he speaks of similarity is not the kind of similarity that occurs in "a wakeful state" – the recognition of an identity between one thing and another. Rather, it is a similarity that belongs to a dream world "in which everything that happens appears not in identical but in similar guise, opaquely similar to itself" (*SW* 2, 239). Benjamin quickly dispels the opaqueness of his own description with the example of a children's game: "children know a token of this world: the stocking, when it is rolled up in the laundry hamper, has the structure of this dream world, it is a purse and a dowry at the same time" (*SW* 2, 239–40). These children, Benjamin continues, do not tire of transforming the purse into a stocking. The rolled up stocking promises, as a purse, to contain a dowry, but the dowry it offers and which the children do not tire of showing is that the promise is not fulfilled. Unrolling the purse reveals that it is a stocking. In *Berlin Childhood around 1900*, Benjamin tells a similar story about himself. His conclusion to this story states what is important in this unrolling of the "purse": "It taught me that form and content, veil and what is veiled, are the same" (*SW* 3, 374). This similarity forms the world for which Proust is homesick: a world in which an image remains undefined by what it promises to reveal. The image does not coincide with what it promises but rather with what it is, a stocking. This deeper similarity emerges as a relation that frees the image from a predetermined meaning, its dowry, its promise of a reality that it cannot fulfill.

This more complex understanding of the image is the basis for Benjamin's interpretation of the *mémoire involontaire* in Proust's novel. In contrast to conscious memory (through which we deliberately recall the past), this is a memory that vividly asserts itself without being sought after. Moreover, when it occurs, it asserts itself to such an extent that it takes over consciousness of the present. This kind of memory, Benjamin points out, is not a simple remembering of the way things were. He writes: "the important thing to the remembering author is not what he experienced, but the weaving of his memory" (*SW* 2, 238). Benjamin first compares this weaving to the work that Odysseus' wife, Penelope, undertook everyday while waiting his return. But, just as Penelope's weaving is unwoven by night so that she may begin again the following day, this weaving of memory is matched by a forgetting. This leads Benjamin to ask: "is not the involuntary recollection, Proust's *mémoire involontaire*, much closer to forgetting than what is usually called memory?" (*SW* 2, 238). This memory is interrupted by forgetting in much the same way as the purse, when it is unrolled into a stocking, interrupts our expectations with the sudden revelation of a non-coincidence between what it appeared to be and what it is. What occurs in the forgetting that belongs to *mémoire involontaire* is an unraveling of the threads of conscious memory, that is, of the kind of memory that understands its images as representations of the past. Forgetting releases memory from dependence on the past. In this release, the significance of the image is no longer rolled up in a preceding event. It is this freedom that allows the true surrealist face of existence to break through. The image is no longer tied to what it represents but rather expresses a discrepancy between what it is and what it appears to be. The expression of such a discrepancy is the meaning of the image in Benjamin's Proust. But this is not all. Because of this discrepancy, the image is no longer required to appear singly (as if its existence were dependent on a single event). Instead, what appears is a train of images – like the train that begins with the bite of a madeleine and sets off an extensive web of memories.

This freeing of the image from a history that has tied it to the contemplation of a singular event is the mark of modern experience for Benjamin. Surrealism sought to express this experience through the montage-like effect Benjamin adopts in *One-Way Street*. Such montage insists that the significance of what we see and read takes place not in the isolation of one image but in the experience of the images that make up the montage as well as how they relate to one another. In Proust, the *mémoire involontaire* demands that its images are experienced in such a way so that they "tell us about a whole, amorphously and formlessly, indefinitely and weightily, in the same way the weight of the fishing net tells a fisherman about his catch" (*SW* 2, 247). Only in its collective relation to other images does the image reveal its significance. Benjamin discretely points to such a meaning at the very beginning of this essay, before its significance can even be grasped: "the image of Proust is the highest physiognomic expression which the irresistibly growing discrepancy between the literary and life was able to assume. That is the moral which justifies the attempt to call forth this image" (*SW* 2, 237). Since the modern experience of the relation between life and the literary is one of a growing discrepancy, the image can no longer assume its previous role of mediating between them – that it is moral. This again is where the surrealist face of existence breaks through. The physiognomy of this face is found in an image whose effect is neither contemplation nor representation but rather the experience of a discrepancy at the center of both. While Benjamin explores the image in relation to this discrepancy in Proust's writing, its significance, as the surrealism essay indicates, is political. Articulating this political aspect of the image, in particular, the image as it emerges in its modern form or physiognomy becomes the task that centers Benjamin's subsequent writing as he moves towards two of the concepts that will define his work in the 1930s: reproducibility and the dialectical image.

Suggested further reading

Carol Jacobs. "Walter Benjamin: Image of Proust." In her *In the Language of Walter Benjamin*. Baltimore: Johns Hopkins University Press, 1999. 39–58.
John McCole. "Benjamin and Proust: Remembering." In his *Walter Benjamin and the Antinomies of Tradition*. Ithaca, NY: Cornell University Press, 1993. 253–79.
Beryl Schlossman. "Proust and Benjamin: The Invisible Image." In *Benjamin's Ground: New Readings of Walter Benjamin*. Ed. Rainer Nägele. Detroit: Wayne State University Press, 1988. 105–17.

"Theories of German Fascism" (1930)

In the parallelogram of forces formed by nature and nation, war is the diagonal.

Although the Proust essay shows little of the political leanings present in both *One-Way Street* and the surrealism essay, "Theories of German Fascism" directly reflects the shift in the contemporary experience of political life brought about by fascism. For Benjamin, the causes of this shift are not to be found directly in the events that document the rise of fascism in Germany. Rather, they are present, symptomatically, in a collection of essays edited by Ernst Jünger under the title *War and Warriors*. As is frequently the case with Benjamin, the review becomes more than a judgment of the work being considered. Indeed, as Benjamin's title suggests, the subject is how the collective endeavor present in these essays relates to the national and historical claims of German fascism.

Benjamin quickly makes clear that he has little sympathy for the views expressed by the contributors to *War and Warriors*. For him, their understanding of war is no more than an anachronistic ideology (*SW* 2, 313) that misses the colossal change technology has brought to war.

Benjamin's focus on technology is present from the beginning of the review. Technology, he writes, repeatedly demands to be justified in our private lives. He then links this definition to war by citing a remark from the right-wing French publication *Action Française*, in which Léon Daudet writes "L'automobile, c'est la guerre." Benjamin offers the following explanation for this rapidly presented constellation of terms: "This surprising association of ideas was based on Daudet's perception that there had been an increase in technological innovations, in power sources, in tempo, and so on that could find no completely finished, adequate use in our private lives yet still they demanded justification" (*SW* 2, 312). The remark is symptomatic of a position Benjamin will analyze in this review, namely, the rejection of technology in favor of things and ideas that can be completely assimilated. However, the proliferation of technological innovations works against such assimilation into private life. Technology in this sense is the shock of the new that cannot quite be absorbed before it is followed by yet another innovation. This failure to be absorbed is precisely the aspect of technology experienced in the course of the First World War. For Benjamin, recognition of this failure to absorb arises from the transformation of the heroic mythologizing which led so many into the reality of gas warfare. Benjamin remarks: "Gas warfare, in which the contributors to this book show conspicuously little interest, promises to give the war of the future a face which will permanently replace soldierly qualities by those of sports; all action will lose its military character, and war will assume the countenance of record setting" (*SW* 2, 313). In Jünger's volume, Benjamin observes, there is no recognition of this transformation of war. In its place there is only a "cult of war."

Benjamin sees this cult aspect as "nothing other than the uninhibited translation of the principles of *l'art pour l'art* to war itself" (*SW* 2, 314). The linking of this cult of war to the principles of an aesthetic movement underscores the kind of understanding Benjamin uncompromisingly takes aim at after the materialist and political turn in his writing. Although the critical project of his earlier writings also sought to escape the grasp of the aesthetic, this took place in the name of discovering the truth-content of a work. Now, that project attains significance from its political consequences. This is why, as Benjamin claims in *One-Way Street*, maintaining a standpoint is no longer relevant to criticism.

The first part of "Theories of German Fascism" reflects the failure of a standpoint to grasp the significance of contemporary experience. Benjamin not only points out how the First World War differs from the heroic struggle of the soldier repeated throughout Jünger's volume but also identifies what produces this difference: technology. While this identification marks the first attempt by Benjamin to provide a significant account of the effect of technology on modern experience, he does not yet assign an explicit political effect to technology as he will later in "The Work of Art in the Age of Its Technical Reproducibility." Rather, he uses the appearance of technological warfare in the First World War to expose the historical distortion present in the cult of war developed by Jünger and the other contributors to *War and Warriors*. At the same time, Benjamin also recognizes that, although technology allows him to expose this distortion, this exposure does not prevent the subsequent use of technology by the ideology he sees embodied in Jünger's volume: fascism.

What Benjamin traces in this review is the effect of a kind of thinking about war that was being appropriated by the fascists. Benjamin is explicit on this point. He observes that Jünger's volume, by presenting war as "the highest manifestation of the German nation" (*SW* 2, 315), is at one with the "new nationalism" of the fascists. The relation between this nationalism and the idealization of the heroic soldier of the First World War is now emphatically stated: "what developed here, first in the guise of the World War volunteer and then in the mercenary of the *Nachkrieg*, is in fact the dependable fascist class warrior. And what these authors mean by 'nation' is a ruling class supported by this caste" (*SW* 2, 319). The irony Benjamin's review reveals is that the fascist nation produced by this cult of war no longer attempts to sustain itself through such heroic warriors but rather through the technologization of war: "war, in the metaphysical abstraction in which the new nationalism believes, is nothing other than the attempt to release, mystically and without mediation, the secret of nature, understood idealistically, through technology" (*SW* 2, 319). Within this nationalism, technology is an instrument whose purpose is to affirm idealistic claims while subjecting nature to its force. War in this context can be justified as an extension of the technological pursuit of the meaning of nature.

According to Benjamin's argument, the appropriation of nature by technology (in the form of war) produces a nationalism that transforms the heroic soldier figure. What then arises is a "fascist nation" that "takes its place as a new economic mystery of nature alongside the old" (*SW* 2, 319). Although the new is driven by the belief that the nation exists in order to wrest this secret from nature, Benjamin notes that what occurs is that "this old mystery of nature, far from revealing itself to their [the fascists'] technology exposes its most threatening feature" (*SW* 2, 319). This feature is nothing less than war: not the idealized heroic war of Jünger's volume, but a mythical war in which technology will produce in the place of the secret of nature "millions of human bodies [that] will indeed inevitably be chopped up to pieces and chewed up by iron and gas" (*SW* 2, 320–21). It is in this sense that Benjamin describes war as the diagonal of a parallelogram formed by the forces of nature and nation: war is the common boundary. It is the diagonal where they meet.

Benjamin could have had no idea of the accuracy of the effect of the marriage of war and technology he predicts here. Yet, even within this dire prediction, Benjamin harbors a positive significance for technology. The positive is reserved for those who "refuse to acknowledge the next war as an incisive magical turning point, and instead discover in it the image of everyday actuality" (*SW* 2, 321). Against war as the "magical turning point" through which Jünger and also fascism sought to recover the German nation, Benjamin places what he had first explored in *One-Way Street*: "the image of everyday actuality." The revolutionary power of this actuality is not in doubt for Benjamin, whose last word in this review calls for such an actuality to "transform this war into civil war, and thereby perform that Marxist trick which alone is a match for this sinister runic nonsense" (*SW* 2, 321). Here, Benjamin expresses his optimism that the revolutionary potential of "everyday actuality" can have an effect on the aestheticizing, mythologizing forces that combine to produce the fascist state.

Suggested further reading

Angsar Hillach. "The Aesthetics of Politics: Walter Benjamin's 'Theories of German Fascism'," *New German Critique* 17 (spring 1979), 99–119.

"Karl Kraus" (pub. 1931)

> Attempt to illustrate the genuinely mediated effectiveness of
> revolutionary writing with reference to the works of Karl Kraus.

Despite the overt engagement with the political history of his time in "Theories of German Fascism," Benjamin still maintained the strong interest in language that appears in his writings between 1916 and 1925. The Kraus essay continues this interest but does so in a way that brings Benjamin's current materialist and political concerns to bear on language. Benjamin had published shorter pieces on Kraus in 1928 and 1929, and, also in 1928, devoted a whole section to him in *One-Way Street*. But this is not the only period of his career that Benjamin gives attention to Kraus. Scholem, in *The Story of a Friendship*, recalls that Benjamin may have started paying attention to Kraus as early as 1916. Certainly by 1919, Kraus and his journal were a topic of conversation between them, as the first reference to Kraus in Benjamin's letters confirms.

Kraus was an Austrian satirist, dramatist, poet, and aphorist who published a widely read journal, *Die Fackel* (The Torch), between 1899 and his death in 1936. He was known as an uncompromising critic of his times – the kind of critic who could deduce the fate of the world from a misplaced comma in a sentence. His satirical attacks were most frequently aimed at the journalism of his time but also at the political corruption of Vienna. Psychoanalysis was also a frequent target – Kraus is responsible for the famous put-down: "Psychoanalysis is the illness for which it claims to be the cure."[5]

Benjamin sees Kraus's attacks against the press as the act of a critic who "brought together all his energies in the struggle against the empty phrase." Such a phrase is further defined as "the linguistic expression of the despotism with which, in journalism, actuality sets up its dominion over things" (*SW 2*, 434). Given the emphasis on actuality in *One-Way Street*, Benjamin's sympathy for Kraus's critique of journalism could be misunderstood. An important difference to bear in mind is that journalism, as the record of actuality, emphasizes events over things. In *One-Way Street*, Benjamin sought to emphasize actuality in the existence of things. This emphasis explains why he is drawn to Kraus's critique of journalism. Kraus attacks the "changed function of language in the world of high capitalism," that is, in the world where the empty phrase makes a thought "marketable" just as events make newspapers marketable (*SW 2*, 435). In this respect, Kraus's writing becomes the setting in which Benjamin can not only uncover the play of market forces and its effect on language but also develop a more materially inflected understanding of language.

In the third section of the essay, Benjamin develops this understanding through his remarks on the instrument of Kraus's critique: quotation. That the method of Benjamin's last major, unfinished work, *The Arcades Project*, is based on the organization of an enormous number of quotations cannot be overlooked here, given that this was a project whose beginnings can be traced to 1926. But, even before embarking on this project, quotation held an attraction for Benjamin. In a 1924 letter, he clearly exults in the 600 quotations he had gathered for the *Origin of the German Tragic Drama* (*C*, 236). By the time of the Kraus essay, this interest in quotation has become more than a source of knowledge or scholarly endeavor: quotation emerges as a montage-like form of discourse capable of possessing a significance beyond the context from which the passage is drawn. In the drafts of the Kraus essay, a sense of this significance is discernible in the admiration that accompanies Benjamin's simple observation that "Kraus has written an article in which not a single word is by him" (*GS* 2, 1093). Underwriting this remark is the recognition that words, once quoted, are both destructive (of their former context) and constructive or creative. However, for Benjamin, the constructive part is not the addition of another meaning for the quoted words. Benjamin writes:

> [Quotation] summons the word by its name, wrenches it destructively from its context, but precisely thereby calls it back to its origin. Not without sense does it appear sonorously [as rhyme], congruously, in the jointure of a new text. As rhyme, it gathers the similar into its aura; as name, it stands alone and expressionless. Before language two realms justify themselves in the quotation – origin and destruction. And conversely, only where they interpenetrate – in citation – is language complete.   (*SW* 2, 454)

In the structure of a new work, quotation calls words back to their origin in language, their origin in the name. The understanding expressed here recalls the 1916 essay "On Language as Such and on the Language of Man" in which Benjamin defines the name as the means by which things and objects can be communicated (the means by which we have knowledge), but he also adds, in that communication, that the name marks the difference between language and things. When quotation summons the word by its name, it summons language to its origin in this difference (without which no communication could occur in language). By being destructively wrenched from their context, the quoted words are thus brought back to that capacity to name in which language originates. Benjamin describes the effect of such quoting by recalling two terms that had important roles in earlier essays: the "similar" from the Proust essay and the "expressionless" from the Goethe essay. In the latter, the expressionless is what completes the work by fracturing it. By becoming name, quotation fractures the relation of words to the context in which they occurred. This fracturing is the destructive aspect of quotation. In the Proust essay, the similar was distinguished from identity in order to convey the sense of the image as something whose meaning does not derive from what it represents. Here, Benjamin's play on the literal and figurative meaning of rhyme comes to the fore: figuratively "rhyme" means sense, as in the English phrase "rhyme and reason"; literally, rhyme indicates a relation of words whose meanings are not identical with one another despite the similarity of their sound. Benjamin brings these two terms together as the defining characteristics of a practice of quotation which he not only sees at work in Kraus but which will also inform the method of the materialist criticism he will develop through the 1930s.

Benjamin's interpretation of the role of quotation in Kraus and his linking of it to the critical and political concerns he was engaged with at this time is perhaps the part of this essay that remained unknown to Kraus. Rather than the redemptive aspect of quotation, the destructive is more strongly at work in Kraus's own writings. By bringing out the former, Benjamin offers less an interpretation of Kraus than an analysis of the significance of his polemical method. Articulating the way in which the redemptive and the destructive are interpenetrated will become a hallmark of Benjamin's subsequent thinking. What Benjamin then discovers in Kraus's use of quotation is "the only power in which hope still resides that something might survive this age – because it was wrenched from it" (*SW* 2, 455). Such wrenching will return as the method of *The Arcades Project* as well as the way in which history happens in Benjamin's last writings.

Suggested further reading

Alexander Gelley. "Epigones in the House of Language: Benjamin on Kraus," *Partial Answers: Journal of Literature and the History of Ideas* 5.1 (2007), 17–32.

Sigrid Weigel. "Eros and Language: Benjamin's Kraus Essay." In *Walter Benjamin: Language, Literature, History.* Ed. Ragnhild E. Reinton and Dag T. Andersson. Oslo: Solum Forlag, 2000. 26–45.

(d) Media and revolution 1931–1936

Between 1931 and 1936 some of Benjamin's most well-known works are completed. Not only does "The Work of Art in the Age of Its Technical Reproducibility" date from this period, but also "Little History of Photography," a first version of an essay on Brecht "What is Epic Theater?," "Experience and Poverty," "Franz Kafka," "The Author as Producer," and "The Storyteller." In addition, during this period, Benjamin works on his autobiographical texts, *Berlin Chronicle* and *Berlin Childhood around 1900*, and publishes a collection of letters by German writers using the pseudonym Detlev Holz in order to avoid the attention of the fascist authorities.

While the essays on photography and the work of art stand out and also frame these years, the issues they raise are also reflected in the writings on more literary subjects. Foremost among these is the possibility of a revolutionary art. New media such as photography in the nineteenth century and cinema in the early twentieth century lend themselves easily to revolutionary claims on the strength of their newness. What Benjamin attempts to secure through these new media is an account of art no longer dependent on contemplation and the aesthetic distance it demands between artwork and audience – precisely the terms in which the auratic character of art will be presented. As a means of displacing this auratic aspect, Benjamin will emphasize the materialist basis of the aesthetic understanding that has been so prevalent in the history of art. The name of this method is dialectical materialism.

Dialectical materialism derives from Marx's materialist concept of history; however, it is not a term used by Marx (nor is historical materialism). In fact, both are coined later within a more theoretical development of Marx's thought. For Benjamin, his encounter with these terms and the thinking they reflect first occurs in 1924 when he reads Lukács's *History and Class Consciousness*. Broadly speaking, the approach of dialectical materialism locates things or the material reality of life within a process that involves ongoing conflict and opposition. Because no absolute power governs this process, its development is dialectical in nature, that is, it proceeds through a movement that registers the changing relations between the different elements of a society as they participate in the material conditions of their existence. Focusing on these conditions permits the analysis of the political, cultural, and intellectual tendencies of an age without succumbing to the ideologies present in that age. Interpreting this dialectical movement in the material of culture is the central task of the project Benjamin undertakes in his writings in the 1930s as he seeks to place the political, cultural, and intellectual forces of his time within a dialectical and materialist understanding of history.

"Little History of Photography" (1931)

The literarization of the conditions of life.

With this essay Benjamin opens the analysis of technology and cultural forms for which he is most widely known. The essay undertakes a "backward glance" at the history of photography. The thesis informing this procedure is that the early years of photography allow Benjamin to recover historical and philosophical questions that "have gone unheeded since its first decades" but which are once again evident. Why these questions went unheeded is attributed to the industrialization of photography. The reason they can now be asked again, Benjamin claims, results from a crisis in capitalist industry. Yet, despite being set within this historical and political frame, the questions posed by this essay provide a more philosophical account of visual perception. The critique of capitalist industry provides a frame, always present in the background; however, it is not developed significantly beyond Benjamin's opening remarks.

The essay quickly moves to distinguish the technological significance of photography from traditional concepts of art. Benjamin underlines how little these concepts have in common with photography and also how great a mistake it is to try and understand photography with them. To do so, Benjamin observes, is to try and legitimize photography "before the very tribunal [it] was in process of overturning" (*SW* 2, 508). The radical divergence between photography and traditional forms of art reflects Benjamin's sense that another nature is at work in photography, a nature that cannot be comprehended by the traditional approach to understanding art.

Benjamin indicates the qualities that make photography distinctive in the following terms:

> No matter how artful the photographer, no matter how carefully posed
> his subject, the beholder feels an irresistible urge to search such a picture
> for the tiny spark of contingency, of the here and now, with which reality
> has (so to speak) seared the subject, to find the inconspicuous spot
> where in the immediacy of that long-forgotten moment the future nests
> so eloquently that we, looking back, may rediscover it.   (*SW* 2, 510)

Like the magical aspect of language Benjamin writes about in 1916, the photograph has a double quality which belongs to it quite independently of the
artfulness of the photographer. This doubleness occurs in the way that two
opposite aspects are present: pastness and immediacy. As the Proust essay also
insists, this pastness occurs as an image. As such, its significance is not to
present the past as it really was. Instead, the photographic image contains a
contingency that only the present is able to recognize. In the case of David
Hill's photograph of a Newhaven fishwife, Benjamin captures this contingency
in the series of questions posed by this image: "there remains something that
goes beyond testimony to the photographer's art, something that cannot be
silenced, that fills you with an unruly desire to know what her name was, the
woman who was alive there, who even now is still real and will never consent
to be wholly absorbed in 'art'" (*SW* 2, 510).

In the technical sphere, Benjamin explains this ability of the photographic
image to reveal a hidden significance through what he calls the optical unconscious, one of the central concepts of this essay. It is described as follows:

> another nature ... speaks to the camera rather than to the eye: "other"
> above all in the sense that a space informed by human consciousness
> gives way to a space informed by the unconscious. While it is a
> commonplace that we have some idea about what is involved in the act
> of walking (if only in general terms), we have no idea at all about what
> happens during the fraction of a second when a person actually takes a
> step. Photography, with its devices of slow motion and enlargement,
> reveals the secret. It is through photography that we first discover the
> existence of this optical unconscious, just as we discover the instinctual
> unconscious through psychoanalysis.   (*SW* 2, 510–12)

The contingency present in the image and the experience of an optical unconscious are effects attributable to the medium of photography. Thus, the
emergence of photography has both historical and perceptual consequences.
Historical, because the significance of an image from the past is no longer determined by the past (the contingency, the here and now of the moment recorded
in the image, can only be uncovered in the future). Perceptual, because aspects

of an object not visible to the human eye are made available to perception. These two aspects are the foundation of Benjamin's account of photography: one points to a contingency that the actuality of a photographic image cannot help but present; the other points to a technological character that distinguishes photography from a history of producing images through human abilities.

These historical and perceptual aspects define the extent to which photography has transformed the relation between the image and its beholder. To explain this transformation, Benjamin introduces the concept with which he is most widely associated: the aura. Benjamin writes:

> What is aura, actually? A strange weave of space and time: the unique appearance of a distance, no matter how close it may be. While at rest on a summer's noon, to trace a range of mountains on the horizon, or a branch that throws its shadow on the observer, until the moment or the hour become part of their appearance – this is what it means to breathe the aura of those mountains, that branch.   (*SW* 2, 518)

The mountains and the branch become auratic as their spatial existence is defined according to a particular moment in time, thereby making what is seen unique. As such, an object appears to the beholder in the form of an image whose significance is locked to a particular time and place. In the case of photography, the opposite is true because the experience of the image is no longer restricted to a specific place and time but can exist in different places at different times yet remain unchanged. Benjamin interprets this aspect of photography as the sign of a change in perception:

> The peeling away of the object's shell, the destruction of the aura, is the signature of a perception whose sense for the sameness of things in the world has grown to the point where even the singular, the unique, is divested of its uniqueness by means of its reproduction.
>
> (*SW* 2, 518–19)

Photography removes the shell from things in the world and brings them to the beholder in a way that emphasizes an experience based on transience and reproducibility. Transient because photography presents objects at a moment in their existence rather than something that has the appearance of a fixed and unique significance. Reproducible because the question of which photographic print is more original than another is irrelevant: a print made ten years ago and one made today are essentially the same. In both these aspects, the photographic image opens up the possibility of a different relation to history as well as a different understanding of history – one in which the material object has a significant role.

For Benjamin, the work of a French photographer, Eugène Atget, exemplifies this different understanding. What attracted Benjamin to Atget's images of deserted Paris streets was the way they separated the material existence of the world from any presence of a human subject. In this respect, Benjamin sees Atget's documentary images of Paris as being at one with the "salutary estrangement between man and his surroundings" typical of surrealist photography. Furthermore, it is in this estrangement that Benjamin discovers the ability of photography to give "free play to the politically educated eye" (*SW* 2, 519).

Benjamin traces the political aspect of the photography practiced by Atget and the surrealists to the more purely technological nature of the camera's means of representation. This is succinctly stated in the later essay on the work of art: "photography freed the hand from the most important artistic tasks in the process of pictorial reproduction, tasks that now devolved solely upon the eye looking into a lens" (*SW* 4, 253). As the hand no longer shapes the image so too does the image relinquish any intimate relation between the human figure and the surroundings it inhabits. Since the aura is recognized because of the way in which an object appears to a human subject, Benjamin sees in Atget a figure who initiated the movement to "emancipate the object from aura" (*SW* 2, 518). Through this emancipation, the political function of photography emerges in a form that brings "a living and unequivocal relationship with modern life" (*SW* 2, 523). Photography achieves this by altering the relation between the human and the material world. No longer does the singular, the individual, and the unique serve as the source of cultural and social meaning. Instead, the material existence of the world opens to the free play of the politically educated eye. Benjamin attributes this opening to a "shock effect [that] paralyzes the associative mechanisms in the beholder" (*SW* 2, 527). The shock in question arises when the beholder is confronted with images of urban landscapes from which the human subject is absent.

Benjamin defines the effect of Atget's photography as "the act of unmasking or construction" (*SW* 2, 526). This definition recognizes that Atget's images of Paris should not be regarded as a merely documentary project, as if their significance could be restricted to merely reflecting reality. Even if Atget had intended this, their effect is quite different. The absence of the human figure indicates for Benjamin (who cites Brecht when making this point) that "something must in fact be *built up*, something artificial, posed" (*SW* 2, 526). In other words, the human connections into which these images are placed must be recognized as constructed. Yet, this recognition is only part of Benjamin's understanding.

Another element also comes into play: inscription. After describing the shock effect that paralyzes the associations of the beholder, Benjamin writes: "This is where inscription must come into play, which includes the photography of the literarization of the conditions of life, and without which all photographic construction must remain arrested in the approximate" (*SW* 2, 527). If the constructive effect of photography were merely the interruption of an auratic response, its achievement would remain negative. To this interruption Benjamin adds the necessity of inscription. A photography that performs this inscription is a photography that performs what Benjamin calls, after Brecht, a literarization of the conditions of life. Brecht's use of this word literarization is related to another concept he developed in these years: *Umfunktionierung*, which means the "re-functioning" of one medium in terms of another.[6] The questions Benjamin poses at the end of this essay all address the effects of this "re-functioning": "Shouldn't a photographer who cannot read his own pictures be no less accounted an illiterate? Won't inscription become the most important part of the photograph?" (*SW* 2, 527). These questions underscore the need to read the material conditions of existence already inscribed within photography. Through them, the questions photography posed at its very beginning return – questions that then also heralded a re-functioning of art. With the recognition of a modern "re-functioning" in this process of inscription, photography reclaims what Benjamin calls earlier in this essay "a living and unequivocal relationship with modern life."

Suggested further reading

Eduardo Cadava. *Words of Light: Theses on the Photography of History*. Princeton: Princeton University Press, 1997.

"The Author as Producer" (1934)

> Commitment alone will not do it.

The "re-functioning" Benjamin introduces in the "Little History of Photography" also figures prominently in "The Author as Producer," one of the most politically committed essays he writes in the 1930s. However, what produces this "re-functioning" is not simply the result of what an author or critic chooses to do. In notes summarizing this essay – which Benjamin writes during his stay with Brecht in the summer of 1934 – he alludes to this "re-functioning" in a way that more strongly identifies its occurrence as a historical effect: "I develop the theory that a decisive criterion of a revolutionary function of literature lies in the extent to which technical advances lead to a change in the function of artistic forms and hence of the intellectual means of production" ("Notes from Svendborg," *SW 2*, 783). These technical advances, now identified as the historical tendency of the modern age, open the door to a political art.

In this essay, Benjamin is well aware of how limited the quality of literature can be when its significance is restricted to a political agenda. For this reason, he begins by carefully distinguishing between two types of author. First, there is the bourgeois author who claims to create from a position of autonomy and freedom. Second, there is the author who recognizes the extent to which the "present social situation" makes it necessary "to decide in whose service he is to place his activity" (*SW 2*, 768). Since the former has always been regarded as a sign of literary quality, the question posed by this distinction is whether the latter can co-exist with the literary. Benjamin's response to this question is an emphatic yes. Accordingly, his intention is "to show that a literary work can be politically correct only if it is also correct from a literary point of view" (*SW 2*, 769). But, instead of placing a political tendency within a literary work, Benjamin reverses expectations and asserts that literary quality is always contained within the political: "this literary tendency, which is implicitly or explicitly contained in every *correct* political tendency of a work, alone constitutes the quality of that work" (*SW 2*, 769). The change announced by this claim is that the literary is no longer the representation of an external political position; rather the literary is political.

This shift in how politics relates to literature is explained by a shift in the kind of question to be addressed to literature. Benjamin writes:

> Rather than asking, "What is the attitude of a work *to* the relations of production of its time?" I would like to ask, "What is its position *in* them?" This question directly concerns the function the work has within the literary relations of production of its time. It is concerned, in other words, directly with the literary technique of works.
>
> (*SW 2*, 770; emphasis added)

The replacement of "to" by "in" suggests a subtle difference, yet the whole essay as well as Benjamin's brand of materialist criticism depends on it. The use of "to" not only affirms a distinction between literature and its political significance but this distinction continues the tradition of making one the representation of the other.

The overcoming of this tradition lies in what Benjamin calls technique. Technique, he explains,

> makes literary products accessible to an immediately social, and therefore materialist, analysis. At the same time, the concept of technique provides the dialectical starting point . . . furthermore, this concept of technique contains an indication of the correct determination of the relation between [political] tendency and [literary] quality, the question raised at the outset. (*SW* 2, 770)

With technique, attention is now focused on an aspect that provides a measure of historical comparison between authors as well as an index to the way in which authors stand within the conditions of their time. Such an approach allows literature to be defined according to the development of techniques that produce a transformation of its forms – in the same way that technology produces a transformation in the way we live our lives. Since technique is a productive force, then, literature can be read as occurring in tandem with the conditions of production prevailing at a given time. These conditions are overwhelmingly technological in the 1930s. As a result, Benjamin's emphasis on technique is an attempt to "rethink our conceptions of literary forms or genres" in order to "identify the forms of expression that channel the literary energies of the present" (*SW* 2, 771). In a more expansive vein, Benjamin explains, "we are in the midst of a mighty recasting of literary forms, a melting down in which many of the opposites in which we have been used to think may lose their force" (*SW* 2, 771). This recasting of literary forms reflects Benjamin's adherence to Brecht's concept of "re-functioning."

Benjamin clarifies the dialectical process at work in this melting down of opposites by referring to a Russian author, Sergei Tretiakov, whose remarks on the decline of writing are cited at length. Here, Benjamin's interest in Kraus's crusade against bad writing takes on its full political significance. Rather than simply attack the decline of writing, Benjamin, feigning to cite a "left-wing author" but actually citing himself, declares that this decline "proves to be the formula for its [writing's] revival" (*SW* 2, 771). In this formula Benjamin perceives a dialectical process at work: the negative (the decline of writing) becomes the foundation for something positive (the redefinition of who can be an author). In conclusion, Benjamin, again citing himself as the "left-wing author," refers to this overcoming of a culture of specialization as "the literarization of the conditions of living" (*SW* 2, 772).

Benjamin had referred to the call for the "literarization of the conditions of life" at the end of the "Little History of Photography"; however, the full political and dialectical consequences of this call only emerge in this essay. Benjamin comments:

> only by transcending the specialization in the process of intellectual production – a specialization that, in the bourgeois view, constitutes its order – can one make this production politically useful; and the barriers imposed by specialization must be breached jointly by the productive forces that they were set up to divide. The author as producer discovers – even as he discovers his solidarity with the proletariat – his solidarity with certain other producers who earlier seemed scarcely to concern him.   (*SW* 2, 775)

The political significance Benjamin attaches to the elimination of specialization is found in its refusal to sustain the kind of bourgeois aesthetics that defines the author as a specialist. Once this specialization is broken down, the author also becomes a producer. The solidarity with the proletariat is then derived from the identity of both as producers.

An immediate consequence of this identity is that artistic production can be reinterpreted in line with the class struggle of Marxist theory. This is precisely the consequence Benjamin now follows:

> If you look back from this vantage point on the recasting of literary forms that I spoke of earlier, you can see how photography and music, and whatever else occurs to you, are entering the growing, molten mass from which the new forms are cast. You will see this confirmed: it is the literarization of all the conditions of life that alone gives an accurate conception of the range of this melting-down process, just as the state of the class struggle determines the temperature at which – more or less perfectly – it is accomplished.   (*SW* 2, 776)

The dissolution of the traditional forms of art is now portrayed in the extended metaphor of industrial production. Since it is a melting process, the literarization or "re-functioning" of art will generate the heat that allows the progress of the class struggle to be measured. Underpinning this metaphor is Benjamin's claim that new productive forms emerge according to a historical logic that mirrors the logic at work in the class struggle – the logic that eventually leads to revolutionary conditions. An imperative of Benjamin's thinking during these years is thus to affirm that advances in the technique of art are as revolutionary as the changes emerging from the growing chasm between different social classes.

After presenting the theoretical link between art and the class struggle, Benjamin devotes most of the remainder of this essay to an example of this link in Brecht's Epic Theater. Benjamin's discussion of Brecht largely follows the remarks he made in his 1931 essay, "What is Epic Theater?" (later revised in 1939; *SW* 4, 302–09). Brecht, Benjamin explains, develops a theater that has learned from the new media of photography, film, and radio, as well as from recent literature by the surrealists. What each of these sources displays is an ability to interrupt the illusion of a reality fostered by narrative devices such as plot. Although Brecht has not yet publicly defined such interruption in terms of alienation (he does not do so until 1936), Benjamin already speaks of Brecht as concerned with "alienating [the public] in an enduring way, through thinking, from the conditions in which it lives" (*SW* 2, 779). By becoming alienated to what it observes, the audience is forced to recognize the contemporary situation to its own existence. Without alienation, such a situation remains concealed because an audience is left to seek satisfaction through the aesthetic contemplation of a work of art.

For Benjamin, the key device producing this alienation is the procedure known as montage, whereby a "superimposed element disrupts the context in which it is inserted" (*SW* 2, 778). Recognizing this disruption reveals what Brecht calls the *gestus*. Brecht uses this term to define the set of relations in which all of the figures on stage not only stand in relation to one another but do so in a way that allows their specific situation to be recognized. In the following passage Benjamin provides an account of the *gestus* as well as an example of how interruption reveals it:

> Brecht's discovery and use of the *gestus* is nothing but the restoration of the method of montage decisive in radio and film, from an often merely modish procedure to a human event. Imagine a family scene: the wife is just about to grab a bronze sculpture and throw it at her daughter; the father is opening the window to call for help. At this moment a stranger enters. The process is interrupted. What appears in its place is the situation on which the stranger's eyes now fall: agitated faces, open window, disordered furniture.   (*SW* 2, 778–89)

The ability to see this scene as something other than a representation of domestic life arises from the appearance of a stranger who has no natural relation to what is played out on stage. The stranger arrests the action in a way that allows it to be seen as a situation in which sympathy for the daughter has no role. Instead, what emerges are questions about what this scene is actually organized around, namely, why the father is at the open window rather than protecting his daughter. Here, the productive process of the theater is revealed to be quite different from any identification with an individual in that scene. Instead, the interruption demands that the audience consider and think about the situation made present by the arrival of the stranger. Because of this demand, the audience participates as a producer rather than a distant, contemplative observer.

Benjamin sees the demand made upon the audience by Brecht's theater as the demand contemporary writers must confront, namely, "the demand *to think*, to reflect on [their] position in the process of production" (*SW* 2, 779). Through this reflection, the solidarity of the writer with the proletariat is located. However, Benjamin adds, the writer remains in a mediated position with regard to the proletariat because the writer, as a member of the intelligentsia, is never really proletarian. Benjamin explains: "the bourgeois class gave him, in the form of education, a means of production that, owing to educational privilege, makes him feel solidarity with it, and still more it with him" (*SW* 2, 780). The result of this situation is that the revolutionary intellectual (here Benjamin cites Louis Aragon, a leader of French surrealism) "appears first and foremost as the betrayer of his class of origin" (*SW* 2, 780). For Benjamin, this betrayal is not a purely destructive task on the part of the writer – in the way that Karl Kraus's satire does nothing more than seek to destroy journalism's reliance on the empty phrase. Benjamin claims that the writer is able to "adapt the productive apparatus to the purposes of the proletarian revolution" (*SW* 2, 780). For Benjamin, the revolutionary role of the writer remains a mediating one yet it is still guided by the attempt to change the function of literature by moving it away from an object contemplated for its beauty at an aesthetic distance. To achieve this, the writer must learn the lessons introduced by photography and film.

These lessons show that the task of the author is no longer defined by the attempt to express spiritual qualities in art. With this last observation, Benjamin clarifies the full political consequences of this essay when he observes that it is through such spiritual qualities that fascism makes itself known. The purpose of the essay is to reclaim the means of production from fascism so that the real political struggle between capitalism and the proletariat can emerge rather than the false struggle between capitalism and spirit invented by fascism for its own political purposes. Defining the author as producer is, therefore, not only an account of the political tendency present in literature but also the opening of the political critique of fascism through a literature and art whose function has already changed with the advent of the technological means of production.

Suggested further reading

Maria Gough. "Paris, Capital of the Soviet Avant-Garde," *October* 101 (summer 2002), 53–83.

"Franz Kafka. On the Tenth Anniversary of His Death" (1934)

> To do justice to the figure of Kafka in its purity and its peculiar beauty, one must never lose sight of one thing: it is the beauty and purity of a failure.

Where Brecht is a positive example of the author as producer, the same cannot be said for Kafka, even when, as Benjamin notes, they both create their art around the use of the gesture. In Kafka, the gestic does not lead to the clarification Brecht sought. Rather, in Kafka's world, Benjamin observes, events become gestures whose meaning remains uncertain. Benjamin explains: "Kafka's entire work constitutes a code of gestures which surely had no definite symbolic meaning for the author from the outset; rather, the author tried to derive such a meaning from them in ever-changing contexts and experimental groupings" (*SW* 2, 801). Benjamin's interest in Kafka focuses on the storytelling in which these contexts and groupings are presented. Kafka's narratives thus unfold as the result of gestures whose meaning is not defined when they occur.

Despite this lack of definition, such gestures still have, for Benjamin, all the quality of an event – so much so that he will insist on seeing the gesture in Kafka as "the decisive thing, the center of the event" (*SW* 2, 802). What is decisive for Benjamin is then an event that not only lacks definite symbolic meaning for the author but, in addition, its meaning is not available to the principal figures who experience them.

Benjamin refers to this inability to penetrate the meaning of the gesture both as an intention of Kafka's writing and as a reflection of what Kafka could least understand in his fiction. Benjamin writes: "Kafka could understand things only in the form of a *gestus*, and this *gestus*, which he did not understand constitutes the cloudy part of the parables" (*SW* 2, 808). This use of gesture produces, according to Benjamin, a narrative art that "regains the significance it had in the mouth of Scheherazade: to postpone the future" (*SW* 2, 807). Kafka's storytelling is therefore suspended between an event stripped of symbolic meaning on the one hand, and, on the other, a future unable to promise another meaning in its place. What remains is then the present, the actuality that Benjamin emphasizes so strongly in his work after *One-Way Street*. But, in the case of Kafka, Benjamin now explores how this appears as the effect of a forgetting.

Benjamin approaches this forgetting by first noting that Kafka "did not consider the age in which he lived as an advance over the beginnings of time." He then goes on to add that Kafka's "novels are set in a swamp world . . . created things appear at the stage which Bachofen has termed the hetaeric stage. The fact that it is now forgotten does not mean that it does not extend into the present. On the contrary: it is actual by virtue of this very oblivion" (*SW* 2, 808–09).[7] The hetaeric stage is defined by Bachofen as a stage of human development that excludes any proof of paternity; however, what interests Benjamin in this aspect of Kafka's writing is that this hetaeric stage is older than the age of myth. Earlier in this essay Benjamin states: "the world of myth is incomparably younger than Kafka's world, which has been promised redemption by myth. But if we can be sure of one thing it is this: Kafka did not succumb to its temptation" (*SW* 2, 799). Kafka's writing then becomes symptomatic of a contemporary world whose modernity is no defense against the seductive promises offered by myth. For Benjamin, Kafka's achievement is to have brought to the fore those forces (from Bachofen's hetaeric stage) that led to the rise of myth as a form of redemption. Still, Benjamin observes, Kafka could neither recognize these forces nor find his way through their effects. Indeed, only in Kafka's posthumous notes is there any kind of recognition of such forces. Benjamin writes,

> only these give some clue to the prehistoric forces that dominated
> Kafka's creativeness, forces which, to be sure, may justifiably be regarded
> as belonging to our world as well. Who can say under what names they
> appeared to Kafka himself? Only this much is certain: he did not know
> them and failed to get his bearings among them.   (*SW* 2, 807)

Benjamin's Kafka does not succumb to the temptation of myth, nor does he recognize the forces that lead to the appearance of myth. In this respect, Benjamin claims that Kafka's relation to his own fiction is comparable to an experience only modern technology can offer. He writes: "experiments have proved that a man does not recognize his own walk on the screen or his own voice on the phonograph. The situation of the subject in such experiments is Kafka's situation" (*SW* 2, 814). Technology not only provides Benjamin with the means to interpret Kafka's situation as an experience of alienation but also marks the difference between Benjamin and Kafka – in the sense that technology permits the recognition of what is at stake both in Kafka's writing and in the actuality of the world in which Benjamin lives.

Benjamin presents what is at stake here when he describes the character of what has been forgotten. He writes, "it is never something individual. Everything forgotten mingles with what has been forgotten of the prehistoric world, forms countless, uncertain, changing compounds, yielding a constant flow of new, strange products" (*SW* 2, 809–10). In a letter written in June 1938, a letter that still reflects the formative effect of the First World War,

Benjamin makes absolutely explicit what this stake means in the modern world of technology:

> What I mean to say is that this reality [technology of modern warfare] can scarcely still be experienced by an *individual,* and that Kafka's world, frequently so serene and so dense with angels, is the exact complement of his epoch, an epoch that is preparing to annihilate the inhabitants of this planet on a considerable scale. The experience that corresponds to that of Kafka as a private individual will probably first become accessible to the masses at such time as they are about to be annihilated.   (*C,* 564)

What Kafka's writing gives voice to is a world from which the individual is so alienated that individuality is no longer an adequate means of experiencing it. The experience of the world then becomes the experience of the mass produced by modern technology. However, such experience only arises from the prospect of annihilation. This is the consequence Kafka could not see and it is also the prospect that informs the need for a different critical response to contemporary experience, a response that refuses not only any mythical or aesthetic promise but also the claim that such experience can be absorbed individually. Benjamin seeks to produce such a response in his revolutionary criticism but, as the development of his thought in the last years of the 1930s reveals most clearly, this criticism is not simply a Marxist derived dialectical materialism, although it remains profoundly influenced by such an approach.

Suggested further reading

Werner Hamacher. "The Gesture in the Name: On Benjamin and Kafka." In Hamacher, *Premises: Essays on Philosophy from Kant to Celan.* Stanford: Stanford University Press, 1996. 294–336.

Hans Mayer. "Walter Benjamin and Franz Kafka: Report on a Constellation." In *On Walter Benjamin: Critical Essays and Recollections.* Ed. Gary Smith. Cambridge, MA: MIT Press, 1988. 185–209.

"The Work of Art in the Age of Its Technical Reproducibility" (1935–1939)

Reproducibility – distraction – politicization.

Benjamin announces in December 1935 that he has finished the first version of what will become his most famous essay, "The Work of Art in the Age of Its Technical Reproducibility." Despite this announcement, revision of the essay continues. By early 1936, there is a second version as well as a French translation (the only form in which the essay is published in Benjamin's lifetime). Finally, there is a third version dating from April 1939.[8] These versions underline the degree to which this essay remained a work in progress. They also reflect the extent to which Benjamin was still searching for an adequate account of the revolutionary potential of contemporary art forms.

When reduced to a programmatic outline, the essay is relatively easy to follow: the function of art changes with the appearance of technology-based art forms such as cinema. The effect of this change is that art is no longer something appreciated by individual contemplation; rather, it is received collectively by a mass audience. Since the cinema creates a new audience for art, it has considerable political consequences for Benjamin. In Marxist terms, cinema sweeps away the traditional function of art in a bourgeois capitalist economy, and, as it does so, it shapes a new form of political participation.

Despite Benjamin's programmatic intentions (expressed most forcefully in the Introduction and the Epilogue), the work of art essay is first and foremost a theory of the historical development of art. Benjamin traces this history of art through the magical and cultic treatment of objects, through the development of a sacred function for these objects in religion, and finally, to the secularization of this sacred function in the cultivation of beauty in art. For Benjamin, such a history is the history of auratic art. In the "Little History of Photography" this auratic aspect was largely defined in terms of distance and the individual contemplation this kind of art required. Here, Benjamin provides a history of the aura not only in order to substantiate its existence but also to establish that the meaning of art is tied to the function it has during a specific historical period. In the case of auratic art, this function affirms values of uniqueness, distance, individuality, contemplation, and authenticity. The last of these, authenticity, is mentioned for the first time in this essay – the other four have been cited in the essay on photography. The appearance of authenticity is, however, less a new development in Benjamin's understanding of this concept than an attempt to define aura with greater specificity.

Benjamin locates authenticity in the "here and now" of an artistic object, that is, in its uniqueness, its inability to be in more than one place at the same time. As such, authenticity is restricted to the original of an artwork. When Benjamin emphasizes that "*the whole sphere of authenticity eludes technological – and, of course, not only technological – reproducibility*" (*SW* 4, 253), he asserts the ability of cinema to allow the same film to be screened simultaneously in London and New York. This is not true for a work defined by authenticity. It has to be in either London or New York. Since the technology of cinema permits the same work to be in two places at the same time, there arises a different perception of what art is. It is no longer dependent on what Benjamin calls "the authority of the object," that is, it no longer depends upon the kinds of attributes that claim autonomy, permanence, uniqueness.

By divesting art of qualities that have long defined its value, Benjamin shifts emphasis to its historical and materialist qualities, that is, to its means of production. In the case of auratic art, a means of production which relies upon the human hand for its creation becomes the basis of their uniqueness and authenticity (no such work can be produced by another hand and be the same). Thus, authenticity is not something a work possesses as some spiritual or aesthetic property; rather, it is an effect of the work's material means of production. Photography, Benjamin writes, was the first medium to do without this concept because it "freed the hand from the most important artistic tasks in the process of pictorial reproduction – tasks that now devolved solely upon the eye looking into a lens" (*SW* 4, 253).

The transformation brought about by photography opens up the political significance of art for Benjamin. At the end of section IV of the essay, he describes this as follows: "*the moment the criterion of authenticity ceases to be applied to artistic production, the whole social function of art is turned about. Instead of having its foundation in ritual, its foundation steps into different practice: namely, its foundation in politics*" (*SW* 4, 256–57, Benjamin's emphasis). These sentences are the first of only three explicit references to politics outside of the Introduction and the Epilogue to this essay. The lack of a direct and sustained treatment of the most important claim of this essay, namely, the political foundation of art in the age of technology, makes the significance of this claim rest squarely on the programmatic intentions expressed in the Introduction to the essay. The emphasis on this programmatic character results in an essay whose significance derives from its prognostic claims rather than from the logical presentation of its ideas.

These prognostic claims first appear in the Introduction when Benjamin claims that the concepts of art introduced by this essay "are completely useless for the purposes of fascism." The concept that gives this essay its title, technical reproducibility, is presented as a means of resisting the use of traditional concepts of art, such as "creativity, genius, eternal value and mystery," which, when used in an uncontrolled way, "allow factual material to be manipulated in the interests of fascism" (*SW* 4, 252). The political stake of the essay is then a theory of art that refuses to be co-opted by fascist methods for manipulating politics according to aesthetic categories. While technology is granted the ability to effect such a refusal, this does not mean that technology is inherently anti-fascist. The Epilogue to this essay points out that technology represents an opportunity whose potential can easily be directed to fascist ends, most notably by war ("Theories of German Fascism" has already pointed this out). However, when the Epilogue repeats such a view of technology (even to the point of reusing phrases from the essay on German fascism), it is now related more explicitly to the aestheticizing tendencies of fascism:

> "Fiat ars – pereat mundus" [Let art flourish – the world pass away] says fascism, expecting from war ... the artistic gratification of a sense perception altered by technology. This is evidently the consummation of *l'art pour l'art*. Humankind which once, in Homer, was an object of contemplation for the Olympian gods, has now become one for itself. Its self-annihilation has reached the point where it can experience its own annihilation as a supreme aesthetic pleasure. *Such is the aestheticizing of politics, as practiced by fascism. Communism replies by politicizing art.*
> (*SW* 4, 270, Benjamin's emphasis)

The fascism Benjamin has described three years earlier as "sinister runic nonsense" is now firmly placed in the context of a history driven and defined by an aesthetic purpose. If technology can be assimilated by such a purpose within fascism, then in what way can concepts arising from the pairing of technology and art be useless to this movement?

First and foremost for Benjamin, cinema presents a different concept of experience. This concept appears when Benjamin observes that "actions shown in a movie can be analyzed much more precisely and from more points of view than those presented in a painting or on the stage" (*SW* 4, 265). Precision of analysis offers a more scientific relation to art, so much so, Benjamin argues, that the separation of artistic from scientific value is no longer sustainable – he explicitly describes this as "one of the revolutionary functions of film" (*SW* 4, 265). The concept of an "optical unconscious" first developed in the essay on photography also belongs to this pairing of science and art. With this concept, Benjamin describes the ability to reveal actions and details the eye cannot perceive and thus provides a different experience of the world. In terms of film, Benjamin locates this experience in the use of close-ups that not only supply "insights into the necessities governing our lives" but open up "a vast and unsuspected field of activity" that counteracts how "our bars and city streets, our offices and furnished rooms, our railroad stations and our factories seemed to close relentlessly around us" (*SW* 4, 265). In these respects, cinema gives an experience that cannot be obtained by human means alone. As a result, it embodies a concept of experience that is not dependent on the human subject. Benjamin's claim is that the removal of the human subject as the only source of experience also removes the source of aesthetic perception manipulated by fascism – aesthetic values and ideas derive from the exercise of an individual subject's judgments about art.

In this context, Benjamin's statement that action in cinema can be analyzed from many more points of view might appear to reinstate the individual subject. However, what is different in this case is that the cinema audience's response is not an effect of the distance that defines the reception of auratic art. In the case of film, Benjamin argues, distance no longer operates because the single defining element in producing this distance – the authenticity conferred by the hand of an individual human subject – has been replaced by a technological means of production. Consequently, there is no elevation of the artwork to an object of veneration distanced from its audience. Once authenticity and its claim to uniqueness is removed, the specialized knowledge needed to judge auratic works also disappears. As a result, Benjamin observes, "in film . . . as in sports . . . everyone is a quasi-expert" (*SW* 4, 262). Here, a Brechtian "refunctioning" of the concept of an expert takes place in a way that recalls the redefinition of the author in Benjamin's "The Author as Producer" (see above). The consequence of this shift away from specialized judgment is that film no longer exerts an auratic hold on its audience. Benjamin explains: "A person who concentrates before a work of art is absorbed by it; he enters into the work, just as, according to legend, a Chinese painter entered his completed painting while beholding it" (*SW* 4, 268). In contrast, a film has to be absorbed by its audience.

Benjamin locates film's ability to deny absorption in the shock effect that arises from how images are presented in cinema: "the train of associations in the person contemplating these images is immediately interrupted by new images. This constitutes the shock effect of film, which, like all shock effects, seeks to induce heightened attention" (*SW* 4, 267). This succession allows no time for contemplation as the film moves from one image to another – in "On Some Motifs in Baudelaire," Benjamin compares this effect in film to the "rhythm of production on a conveyor belt" (*SW* 4, 328). An immediate effect of this shock is that the means of production is experienced without distance by the audience. As a result, the auratic model demanded by painting, an individual contemplating an object, is gone. In its place, there occurs a reception that has a wider social impact. Here, too, a central issue in "The Author as Producer" returns. However, in this later analysis of how art relates to political groupings such as the proletariat, the emphasis is no longer on the parallel between the author and workers as the necessary link. Art itself has now provided the link, through its ability to develop a form that directly relates to the masses in a way that the intellectuals in "The Author as Producer" struggled to do.

Benjamin explains the broader social impact of cinema by emphasizing how its reception occurs in a collective way. In the cinema, Benjamin observes that the responses of its individual audience members form a mass to the extent that they "regulate one another" (*SW* 4, 264). For example, the laughter of some individuals at a particular moment in a film may precipitate a general response from the audience – or even the reverse, an audience may silence this response by not repeating it. The effect of this regulation, he continues, is a "simultaneous collective reception" (*SW* 4, 264). In Benjamin's eyes, what is political about this mode of reception is that it forms a collectivity without the intervention of an individual leader – or Führer. As a result, it embodies a kind of social and political organization different from the one manipulated by fascism.

In the last section of the essay, Benjamin acknowledges that such a change cannot be forced upon its audience lest this result in resistance. This is where he develops his theory of distraction in order to explain how film transmits a new kind of perception that has political significance. (Here, it should be noted that distraction [*Zerstreuung*] also carries the meaning of entertainment.) However, in order to explain how distraction transmits a new mode of perception, Benjamin turns away from cinema and invokes the example of architecture.

For Benjamin, the relevance of this example resides in the two modes of reception demanded by buildings: "by use and by perception. Or, better: tactilely and optically" (*SW* 4, 268). Subsequently, he emphasizes the tactile and, in particular, its crucial element: habit. The tactile aspect arises from the way in which we use buildings: our bodies are in direct contact with them. At the same time, Benjamin argues, this use occurs through habit, that is, it occurs through a means that involves no perception of what a building is – perception is the property of the optical relation to architecture. This contrast between optical and tactile reception sets the stage for Benjamin's explanation of how the demands made by film are mastered by its mass audience:

> *The tasks which are put before the human apparatus of perception at historical turning points are not solved by solely optical means and therefore not by contemplation. They are mastered gradually, under the guidance of tactile reception, through habit.* (*SW* 4, 268; Benjamin's emphasis)

Under the cover of distraction, revolutionary political and social meaning is transmitted by art. In this claim, a fundamental principle of Benjamin's theory of art is present: the task of art is political, that is, its purpose is to create a collective based on a new mode of perception and it performs this task through its capacity for distraction. Why distraction is necessary, Benjamin explains, is because individuals are tempted to evade new modes of perception.

Despite the important role played by distraction in communicating a new mode of perception without arousing resistance or evasion, its success remains in the balance. Film, we are told, "*comes towards* this form of reception by virtue of its shock effects" (*SW* 4, 269; emphasis mine) but what remains undecided in Benjamin's theory of art is whether art can actually affirm the task given to it. This explains both the programmatic nature of the essay as well as Benjamin's optimism that concepts useless to fascism could make a political difference to fascism. Benjamin gives some recognition of this issue when he writes that "it has always been one of the primary tasks of art to create a demand whose hour of full satisfaction has not yet come" (*SW* 4, 266). Benjamin's response to this recognition is to try and justify the revolutionary character of this demand by tracing a tendency within the history of art (its tendency to move away from aura and towards reproducibility). In this regard, art is presented by Benjamin as a means of preparing social and political changes by transmitting the new mode of perception that lies at the base of those changes. Such an art is political to its core since it is the means through which social and political change is mediated in advance of its actual occurrence. By facilitating this mediation, distraction then emerges as the single most important concept in this essay. Not only does distraction transmit new tasks but in doing so it gives art an active political meaning. Here, the "fundamental principles of materialistic art theory" (*C*, 516) Benjamin claims to have discovered emerge: material changes in the media of art are not reflections of political or social changes but rather perform the "directing, instructing stance" (*SW* 2, 777) that defines the political tendency of art in "The Author as Producer." Benjamin's theory of art is an account of such a tendency as it manifests itself in the contemporary direction of art.

Suggested further reading

Marcus Bullock. "The Rose of Babylon: Walter Benjamin, Film, Theory, and the Technology of Memory," *MLN* 103.5 (1988), 1,098–1,120.

Howard Eiland. "Reception in Distraction." *Boundary 2* 30.1 (2003), 51–66.

Eva Geulen. "Under Construction: Walter Benjamin's 'The Work of Art in the Age of Mechanical Reproduction.'" In *Benjamin's Ghosts: Interventions in Contemporary Literary and Cultural Theory*. Ed. Gerhard Richter. Stanford: Stanford University Press, 2002. 121–41.

Miriam Hansen. "Benjamin, Cinema and Experience: 'The Blue Flower in the Land of Technology,'" *New German Critique* 40 (Winter 1987), 179–224.

"The Storyteller" (1936)

> Half the art of storytelling [is] to keep a story free from explanation.

In the same year Benjamin completes the early versions of "The Work of Art in the Age of Its Technical Reproducibility," he also completes this essay on the Russian author Nikolai Leskov (1831–95), a novelist and contemporary of Tolstoy and Dostoevsky. While the essay focuses on Leskov, its true significance lies in Benjamin's development of earlier reflections on storytelling he had written down between 1928 and 1933 in an unpublished piece, "Little Tricks of the Trade" (*SW* 2, 728–30). What Benjamin develops more fully in "The Storyteller" is a concept of experience that also provides this essay's most significant link to Benjamin's thinking in this period.

In 1933, he had also written directly on the relation between a poverty of experience and the loss of storytelling (see "Experience and Poverty" [*SW* 2, 731]). Not only will some of the remarks from this 1933 essay be repeated here but one of the questions posed in this earlier essay makes explicit what is at stake in "The Storyteller": "What is the value of all our cultural capital if it's divorced from experience?" (*SW* 2, 732). Here, experience is not confined to what an individual encounters in the present, but rather it has both an individual and a collective aspect. It is the means by which an individual relates to collective experience. The German word Benjamin uses confirms this: *Erfahrung*. Unlike another word for experience, *Erlebnis*, which refers to experience as something lived or witnessed, *Erfahrung* emphasizes the sense of a wisdom drawn and communicated from experience. An appreciation of the distinction can be gained in English if experience (in the sense of what is handed on from one person to the next) is contrasted with experiences.

In "Experience and Poverty" the relation between the individual and the collective is defined as "communicable experience . . . that passes from mouth to ear" (*SW* 2, 731–32). In this essay, Benjamin traces the interruption of such a relation to the effect of the First World War and the increased use of technology as a means of war. Both have led to a poverty of experience that is termed "a new kind of barbarism." The barbarism Benjamin perceives here is, however, understood in a positive way since its recognition permits a fresh start free from the illusions of the age. Benjamin sees this new start exemplified in the kind of architecture practiced by Paul Scheerbart. Scheerbart's new glass-covered dwellings are also the occasion for one of Benjamin's eminently quotable phrases: "Objects made of glass have no 'aura'" (*SW* 2, 734). The significance of this remark lies in the way it points to the use of opaque walls as an affirmation of privacy and the possession of inwardness as social values. The political and historical meaning of these values is then found in their assertion of the primacy of individual experience. Against the distance that asserts this primacy, Benjamin expresses the hope that the individual, despite the poverty of experience afforded by opaque walls, can still have a relation to the masses (*SW* 2, 735).

Although pursuing the goal of such a relation, the constructive aspect of a poverty of experience is emphasized less in "The Storyteller." Instead, Benjamin's account of the art of storytelling is the analysis of an art whose disappearance is interpreted as a symptom of larger forces, "the secular productive forces of history" (*SW* 3, 146). As Benjamin admits in a letter to Adorno, this disappearance is to be understood in relation to his treatment of aura in the work of art essay: "I have recently written a piece on Nicolai Leskov, and although it does not remotely claim the range of my writings on the theory of art, it does reveal certain parallels to the thesis concerning 'the decline of aura' in so far as I emphasize that the art of story-telling is approaching its end" (*AB*, 140). Storytelling, like the aura, can only be recognized as it disappears. This is the parallel that Benjamin emphasizes.

While Benjamin's essay reveals admiration for the lost art of storytelling as well as a certain nostalgia for its passing, it would be a mistake to see this essay as contradicting his position in the work of art essay. Benjamin distinguishes storytelling from the kind of values associated with auratic art, values that the reproducibility essay seeks emancipation from. For Benjamin, storytelling offers a "communicability of experience" that is received collectively (*SW* 3, 146). In this respect, like cinema, storytelling also offers a collective experience. So too did the epic before such experience declined with the rise of the novel and, later, with the ascendancy of the newspaper.

In the case of the novel, this decline first owes its origin to two material causes: the printing press and the invention of the book. These causes allow the novel to develop as a form created by the isolated individual:

> The storyteller takes what he tells from experience – his own or that reported by others. And he in turn makes it the experience of those who are listening to his tale. The novelist has secluded himself. The birthplace of the novel is the individual in his isolation, the individual who can no longer speak of his concerns in exemplary fashion, who himself lacks counsel and can give none.   (*SW* 3, 146)

From this basis, the novel developed in such a way that it carried to an extreme "the representation of human life" and all its perplexity. For Benjamin, this extreme form integrates "the social process with the development of a person." In so doing, it "bestows the most brittle justification on the order determining that process." He then concludes, "the legitimizing of this order stands in direct opposition to its reality" (*SW* 3, 146–47). Any legitimizing of reality based on individual experience is false to Benjamin. Rather, what is real is formed by the relation of the individual to the collective, which is precisely what he sees occurring in modern experience with film.

Despite the significant role played by the novel in this decline, it is not the decisive form that threatens to bring storytelling to an end. That role is reserved for a form of communication that has even less to do with experience in the sense of *Erfahrung*: the newspaper. Here, the social and political aspect of Benjamin's account of the decline of storytelling emerges:

> With the complete ascendancy of the middle class – which in fully developed capitalism has the press as one of its most important instruments – a form of communication emerges which, no matter how ancient its origins, never before decisively influenced the epic form. But now it does exert such an influence. And ultimately it confronts storytelling as no less of a stranger than did the novel, but in a more menacing way; furthermore, it brings about a crisis in the novel. This new form of communication is information.   (*SW* 3, 147)

Benjamin views the newspaper as the diametrical opposite of the story. In this position, it menaces storytelling more than the novel. Where the story "does not expend itself," the newspaper "does not survive the moment in which it was new" (*SW* 3, 148). The shift in experience from story to newspaper is now cast in political terms: it results from the rise of a bourgeois class created and sustained by capitalism. Against this shift, Benjamin holds up the example of a story that "preserves and concentrates its energy and is capable of releasing it even after a long time" (*SW* 3, 148). His emphasis on these properties reveals the outlines of the historical thinking Benjamin develops in his final years. According to this thinking, the past awaits its significance just as the story awaits the moment in which its significance can be recognized. But another aspect that Benjamin will subsequently develop also surfaces here: the full meaning of storytelling becomes visible in its disappearance – a condition the aura also shares. This condition underlines the extent to which only the present can understand the past and only then as it disappears. In that disappearance, the past is preserved for the time in which its significance can be recognized – what Benjamin will subsequently call the "now of recognizability." Here, Benjamin's late thinking on history takes up the task of the story, to communicate the past as something that has to be told and experienced as the present.

Suggested further reading

Richard Wolin. The Disintegration of Experience. From "Benjamin's Materialist Theory of Experience," in *Theory and Society* 11.1 (1982), 21–27.

(e) History, materialism, and the messianic 1936–1940

The one work that stands over Benjamin's last years is his project on the Paris arcades. Begun in 1927, this project expanded into a massive undertaking that remained unfinished at the time of his death in 1940. This collection of quotations, interspersed with commentary and reflections, which we now know as *The Arcades Project*, has become the epitaph of a career whose contemporary significance owes much to the essays he derived from this project during the 1930s.

The most important of these essays belong to yet another unfinished project, the book on Baudelaire which had the working title of *Charles Baudelaire: A Lyric Poet in the Age of High Capitalism*. In addition, a collection of fragmentary remarks on Baudelaire, entitled "Central Park," ongoing revisions of the reproducibility essay, and his last reflections on history, "On the Concept of History," all remain works in progress at the time of his death. The most notable exception to this record of unfinished projects is the second of his Baudelaire essays, "On Some Motifs in Baudelaire," which the journal of the Institute for Social Research published in early 1940. Other published work from this period includes "Eduard Fuchs, Collector and Historian" and "Problems in the Sociology of Language" – both in the Institute's journal. In addition, a revision of his 1931 essay on Brecht – "What is Epic Theater?" – appears in print (some of the main points of this essay having already been presented in "The Author as Producer"). This essay and the reviews Benjamin completed in this period appear in German journals that, like Benjamin, were also in exile. One exception is "Germans of 1789" which appeared in a French publication. This work repeats the format of "German Men and Women," the collection of letters Benjamin published in 1936 in Germany as a book under the pseudonym Detlev Holz in order to avoid censorship. This second volume is aimed at the stifling of intellectual expression in contemporary Germany.

Despite the statement made by "Germans of 1789," it is *The Arcades Project*, the Baudelaire essays, and the theses on history that provide the defining character of Benjamin's last writings.

The Arcades Project (1927–1940; unpublished)

The theater of all my struggles and all my ideas.

No work in Benjamin's *œuvre* is more fabled than *The Arcades Project*. Conceived in 1927 as a single essay "that will take just a few weeks" (*C*, 322), it increased in significance as Benjamin gathered more and more materials. Despite his research, Benjamin could only state in 1936 that "not a syllable of the actual text exists, even though the end of preparatory studies is now within sight" (*C*, 527). Benjamin continued to work on these studies until he fled Paris in spring 1940. What remains of this project is an immense collection of notes divided and organized into different sections known as "convolutes." Each convolute corresponds to one of the principal subjects under which Benjamin organized his research, such as "Fashion," "Boredom," "Panorama," "Mirrors," "Flâneur," "Baudelaire," and so on. Each convolute is dominated by quotations removed from their contexts and placed in montage-like relation to each other. Interspersed amongst these are notes and observations made by Benjamin. Beyond this organization, it is difficult to say precisely what Benjamin had in mind for the final form of this work. Apart from the two summaries Benjamin prepared for the Institute for Social Research (the Exposés of 1935 and 1939), this mass of notes did not assume a discursive form, although parts do appear in his Baudelaire essays. Moreover, the different treatment of key aspects of this project in the two exposés underlines the extent to which Benjamin still sought to define the theoretical and critical ground of this project. In the end, the unfinished state of *The Arcades Project* may have less to do with his ability to organize the mass of materials collected for this project than with the methodological question posed by the nature of the project itself: the question of actualizing the philosophical and the theoretical in a politically effective form.

Whether a discursive form was even intended for this project is also a matter of debate. Adorno, writing in 1950, asserted that Benjamin's intention was to produce a work consisting "solely of quotations," a work that would "eliminate all overt commentary" so that the meaning can emerge "through a shock-like montage of the material."[9] Despite Adorno's certainty, there is no definite indication of what the final form of this project would have been. The closest

Benjamin comes to such an indication is when, in Convolute N, he states the intention "to carry over the principle of montage into history" (*AP* N2, 6). A similar remark occurs when he describes the theory of this work, he writes that it "is intimately related to that of montage" (*AP* N1, 10). However, there is no explicit indication on Benjamin's part that the presentation will literally become a montage of quotations. His book on the German mourning play can be considered an example here. According to one of his letters, the *Origin of the German Tragic Drama* is a mosaic composed from over six hundred quotations. The example of this earlier book suggests that it might be an error to literalize the principle of montage as the final manner of presentation for this project.

The essays derived from the Arcades material, such as "A Little History of Photography" and his writings on Baudelaire in the late 1930s, provide a strong indication that this collection of quotations could be transformed into discursive writing. However, they do not fully answer the question of what shape *The Arcades Project* would finally assume. Nor do they answer the theoretical and practical questions posed by this work – not the least of which is the relation of theory to practice and the relation of theory to the material objects it interprets. What *The Arcades Project* does offer are the concepts, topics, and figures through which Benjamin sought to resolve the problems posed by these questions, most notably phantasmagoria and commodity fetish on the one hand and, on the other, awakening, the dialectical image, the constellation, and now-time.

(i) Phantasmagoria and commodity fetish

For Benjamin, the construction of the Parisian arcades after 1822 marks the coming together of a capitalist economy with the dominant technological advance of the age: the use of iron in architectural construction. This joining of forces led to an unprecedented ability to display manufactured goods, so much so that the Arcades took on the character of a fairyland – as the title of the essay Benjamin originally planned to write reflects: "Paris Arcades: A Dialectical Fairyland." This fairyland subsequently becomes a phantasmagoria, a dreamworld created by the arcades as a means of sustaining an economy based on the consumption of commodities. The arcades thus provide a concrete example of the moment in which the relation between capitalism and the world of dreams is revealed. In order to analyze this relation and its consequences, Benjamin seeks to gather more and more examples of its "smallest and most precisely cut components" in order to discover what he calls "the crystal of the total event" (*AP* N2, 6).

What Benjamin aims at in this total event is less a history of the age than a shaping of history by the age. That is why he will speak of this project as the attempt "to grasp the construction of history as such" (*AP* N2, 6). Central to this task is the analysis of the phantasmagorical in all its aspects. These aspects include the display and sale of love in prostitution as well as the layout of the modern city of Paris through Haussmann's construction of wide thoroughfares leading to vistas and images as if the city were a huge outdoor art gallery. Defined by such phantasms, the city becomes the place of a dream that extends the forces at work in the arcades into every aspect of experience. Here, what emerges as the total event for Benjamin is the phantasmagoric nature of modernity as it develops within the demands of a capitalist economy.

Benjamin's understanding of this development of modernity is influenced greatly by Lukács's account (which Benjamin first read in 1924 while in Capri) of Marx's analysis of commodity fetishism in the opening chapter of *Capital*. After defining commodity fetishism as the way in which social relations between individuals are displaced into objects, Marx goes on to characterize the result of this displacement as the point when social relations enter the realm of the fantastic. The fantastic arises as the fetishized object takes on a value unrelated to its material existence. The object subsequently begins to take on a life of its own. This transformation of social relations into objects of fantasy informs what Benjamin calls "the new dream-filled sleep" that "came over Europe" (*AP* K1a, 8). Through this sleep, the mythical thought modernity claims to have overcome is reactivated. Benjamin regards the emergence of the arcades in Paris as the embodiment of this reactivation.

Marx is not the only influence present in Benjamin's analysis. Freud's account of erotic fetishization also plays a role. As the arcades display objects whose novelty responds to modernity's appetite for whatever is new, the dream that fuels erotic possession comes into play as human sexual relations are also displaced into objects. These objects, once possessed, only inflame the desire of the consumer to possess yet another object. Here, the place of the prostitute as well as the place of fashion in Benjamin's analysis becomes clear. Both promise a possession that the experience of possessing denies: the prostitute who is transformed into a commodity and fashion which transforms human desire into a desire for what is lifeless (fabric, etc.). By coupling "the living body to the inorganic world," Benjamin notes, "fashion defends the rights of the corpse." Fashion's ability to do so relies upon its presentation of the inorganic as something possessing "sex appeal." In this way, fashion sustains fetishism as "its vital nerve" (*AP* B9, 1) because it is only in the fetish (confusing human significance with an object) that what is inorganic or dead can claim the attention of the living.

The development of a phantasmagoric world fueled by fetish is the total event this project aims to capture. In doing so, Benjamin seeks what he calls the "primal history of the nineteenth century" (*AP* N3a, 2). The purpose of producing this history is not a recovery of the past. Benjamin views this approach as the "strongest narcotic of the century" (*AP* N3, 4). Rather, Benjamin's intention is to liberate "the enormous energies that are bound up in the 'once upon a time' of classical historiography" (*AP* N3, 4). Two goals are intertwined in this intention: the first aims at the awakening of modernity from the dream world into which it has plunged; the second aims at a total reconception of the way history is both written and understood.

Sustaining these goals becomes the source of the methodological problems Benjamin encounters as his work on *The Arcades Project* progresses. These problems cannot be simply attributed to the unfinished state of this project. Nor can they be resolved in a montage of quotations. So much was at stake for Benjamin in this project that it is inconceivable he would have trusted its reception to the kind of presentation Adorno claimed was his intention. Not only was the significance of the past at stake but also the problem of actualizing that past in a way capable of releasing a revolutionary potential in the present. It is precisely the problem of this actualization that informs the most crucial of the concepts Benjamin develops in relation to this project: the dialectical image.

(ii) Awakening and the dialectical image

In his work for *The Arcades Project*, Benjamin recognizes that setting another world in opposition to the dream world created by the nineteenth century will provide no release from its hold. This recognition helps explain why the Marxism present in Benjamin's work has so frequently been viewed as unconventional. Rather than defining a Marxist position in opposition to the commodity fetishism of the nineteenth century, Benjamin is well aware of the need to recognize that the milieu within which "Marx's doctrine arose affected that doctrine." Accordingly, *The Arcades Project* will have to "show in what respects Marxism, too, shares the expressive character of the material products contemporary with it" (*AP* N1a, 7). Although deeply influential for this project, Marxism alone cannot provide the methodological resolution of the issues Benjamin raises. As Benjamin states here, Marxism cannot be abstracted from this age and then be used to critique it from the outside. Accordingly, Benjamin announces another approach: "only with cunning, not without it, can we work free of the realm of the dream" (*AP* G1, 7). If cunning is the only course open to Benjamin, it is because the problem he faces is how to work free of the realm of dream without succumbing to it once more. The dream world must be tricked into revealing its construction. Here, the principle of montage will have an effect since, by placing quotations in relation to one another, they are made to reveal a significance that remains hidden when they are cited alone.

Given that Benjamin describes the nineteenth century in terms of a dream world, it is not surprising to find that his attempt to resolve this problem privileges the moment of awakening. An entry from Convolute N shows the important role played by this moment as well as the significance of his studies on Proust and surrealism to *The Arcades Project*:

> Is awakening perhaps the synthesis of dream consciousness (as thesis) and waking consciousness (as antithesis)? Then the moment of awakening would be identical with the "now of recognizability" in which things put on their true – surrealist – face. Thus, in Proust, the importance of staking an entire life on life's supremely dialectical point of rupture: awakening.   (*AP* N3a, 3)

Like the tearing of a quotation from its context, the moment of awakening is a rupture that Benjamin associates with surrealism. In 1929, he described the "true surrealist face" of this rupture as "a world distorted in the state of similarity" (*SW* 2, 240). Now, however, Benjamin emphasizes the temporal nature of this rupture when he focuses on the moment in which it takes place: the "now of recognizability." The surrealist face that appears here occurs as an awakening in which two opposed states are present. This awakening is neither dream nor waking consciousness. Rather it is a synthesis of both. As such, it combines both the past and what is to come, but does so without being one or the other. Why Benjamin attaches so much importance to the surrealist movement here is because it was the first movement to expose the dream-like relation to objects that emerged in the nineteenth century. Yet, for Benjamin, the surrealists' recognition is also limited since, as his essay on this movement shows, they failed to realize its revolutionary claims. *The Arcades Project* is the attempt to realize that revolutionary potential by adopting a materialist presentation of history. In Benjamin's words, the purpose of this presentation is to "lead the past to bring the present into a critical state" (*AP* N7a, 5). The moment of awakening emphasized by Benjamin is where this critical state is to be realized; it is the moment at which history emerges from the dream of a continuity between past and present and, above all, from the dream that history is a record of progress.

The critical state referred to by Benjamin is not one in which the past casts light on the present, or the present on the past. Rather, this critical state arises from an image formed by the past and the present. In this image, the past and the present occur in a relation that Benjamin calls a constellation. In Benjamin's words: "It is not what is past that casts its light on what is present, or what is present its light on what is past; rather, the image is where what has been comes together in a flash with the now to form a constellation" (*AP* N2a, 3). The term Benjamin uses here, constellation, had already figured importantly in the preface to his *Origin of the German Tragic Drama*. In both cases, the constellation is not a natural formation but one that is only visible from a specific position. In *The Arcades Project*, this formation occurs as a dialectical relation in which past and present are set against one another. The manner in which this takes place (in a flash) emphasizes a suddenness that excludes any predetermination and prohibits continuity with whatever follows. This is why Benjamin describes such an image as "dialectics at a standstill." Past and present are brought together dialectically, but this kind of dialectical relation does not allow itself to be enveloped in an ongoing history or narrative. Such narratives are brought to a standstill, thereby allowing the montage of past and present to be recognized. This montage then allows the unperceived significance of the past to appear as a force in the present. In the case of the arcades, what appears is a recognition of the fetishism through which the revolutionary potential of the new is muted and transformed into yet another commodity available for exchange. As Benjamin makes clear, such recognition can only occur once modernity's complicity with myth and delusion under capitalism has been uncovered. The dialectical image is the means by which Benjamin removes such complicity with myth while he rescues for the present the revolutionary potential that remains hidden in the past.

Benjamin's concept of the dialectical image represents an utterly different way of thinking about the meaning of history. In its montage-like structure, the significance of something from the past is no longer tied to what is already known or written about it. At the same time, this meaning is not available to the past. A quotation from Convolute N provides an example of what Benjamin means here: "'Many pages in Marivaux and Rousseau contain a mysterious meaning which the first readers of these texts could not fully have deciphered'" (*AP* N15a, 1). Compressed here is the understanding that in the past there lies a meaning that can only be recognized at a particular point in the future. This moment is what Benjamin calls the "now of recognizability." It is the moment in which the past and the present enter suddenly into a constellation with each other. Such constellations do not occur at just any moment. Nor are they the product of a more advanced ability to interpret the past. Rather, they are the product of a present that is ready to receive a meaning that the past could not realize. Only in this way can the dialectical image be seen as a synthesis of the past with the present.

Benjamin's favored image for how this moment occurs is the lightning flash. This analogy captures the suddenness and shock effect of how the image appears but also reveals its temporal brevity. As in lightning, appearance and disappearance occur at the same time. In this way, lightning embodies the nature of the "standstill" Benjamin associates with the dialectical image. Just as lightning breaks across the sky, the dialectical image interrupts the flow of a history that has been content to settle into not just sleep but also the dream world of the arcades. Against such a history, the dialectical image is an expression of discontinuity and its critical effect is a direct result of this discontinuity. But what this discontinuity also means is that Benjamin's historical understanding can only be articulated within the dream that fell over Europe in the nineteenth century. Benjamin recognizes that he can only challenge the nexus of history and commodity fetishism in a moment whose critical force demands the colossal actualization of the dream world it seeks to explode apart. This emphasis on the momentary duration of the dialectical image also explains why Benjamin continually speaks in terms of "revolutionary potential." By disappearing like a flash of lightning, these moments define political, revolutionary critique as something whose greatest significance lies in its potential rather than in its actualization. At the same time, the emphasis on the momentary recognizes the danger that confronts all revolutionary politics: falling back into the very history and myths it seeks to dispel. By refusing temporal duration for his most radical historical concept, Benjamin reveals the extent to which the significance of his project on the Paris arcades lies in its theoretical claims. This also accounts for why his most important concept, the dialectical image, possesses so few actual examples. Its critical force lies in a promise that revolutionary history cannot sustain. Its significance is its interruptive force. To actualize this image and sustain it beyond the moment when it flashes before us would be to rob it of this force. For this reason, the most searching historical insight of *The Arcades Project* may also be the reason why this project derives its greatest significance from a failure to achieve its theoretical potential.

Suggested further reading

Susan Buck-Morss. *The Dialectics of Seeing.* Cambridge, MA: MIT Press, 1989.
Beatrice Hanssen, ed. *Walter Benjamin and the Arcades Project.* London: Routledge, 2003.
Rolf Tiedemann. "Dialectics at a Standstill." In Walter Benjamin, *The Arcades Project.* Boston: Belknap, 1999. 929–45.

Richard Wolin. "Experience and Materialism in Benjamin's *Passegenwerk.*" In
    Benjamin: Philosophy, Aesthetics, History. Ed. Gary Smith. Chicago:
    University of Chicago Press, 1989. 210–27.

Charles Baudelaire: A Lyric Poet in the Age of High Capitalism (1937–1939)

> I'm allowing my Christian Baudelaire to be carried into heaven by
> nothing but Jewish angels.

Benjamin had been long familiar with the nineteenth-century French poet
Charles Baudelaire. In 1923, he published translations of his poetry prefaced by
the essay "The Task of the Translator." In the 1930s, he devoted an important
part of his research for *The Arcades Project* to Baudelaire. In July 1937, he
announces a separate book-length study of Baudelaire to be called *Charles
Baudelaire: A Lyric Poet in the Age of High Capitalism.* Despite its conception
as a separate work, Benjamin sees the Baudelaire book as one in which "the
most important motifs of the *Arcades* project converge" (*C*, 556). With this
intention, the Baudelaire project indicates, at least in part, one way in which
Benjamin seeks to develop materials he has collected from his research on
the Paris arcades. At the same time, this intention poses a predicament. If,
as Benjamin claims in a letter to Max Horkheimer in September 1938, his
Baudelaire book "is meant to set down the decisive philosophical elements
of the arcades project in what I hope will be its definitive form," then, this
book raises a question about what will remain of that project beyond a more
expansive presentation of this study of Baudelaire.

Benjamin conceives his study of Baudelaire in three parts with the following
titles: "Baudelaire as Allegorist," "Paris of the Second Empire in Baudelaire,"
and "The Commodity as a Subject of Poetry." The first and third parts were
never completed and exist only as fragments. The second part, entitled "Paris
of the Second Empire in Baudelaire," is first completed in September 1938.
However, as a result of criticisms by Adorno, Benjamin substantially revises
the essay under a new title, "On Some Motifs in Baudelaire." This revision
is published by the Institute in early 1940. Together these essays reveal the
predicament posed by *The Arcades Project.* The first assembles a wealth of
historical material in order to introduce the subjects that will be treated in
the Baudelaire book. The second attempts to produce the theoretical understanding that gives significance to the material in the first essay. Two things
become clear from the history of these Baudelaire essays: first, montage-like

presentation is not enough; and, second, the theoretical resolution of the materials he has collected still remained a question.

(i) "Paris of the Second Empire in Baudelaire" (1937–1938)

To show Baudelaire as he is embedded in the 19th century

Like the book to which it belongs, this essay is written in three sections: "The Bohème," "The Flâneur," "The Modern." Each section of the essay is conceived independently, since Benjamin's intention is not to provide a theoretical account of the historical forces at work in both Baudelaire and the Second Empire – the period 1852–70, when France took an anti-parliamentary turn and was ruled once again by an emperor in the figure of Napoleon III. Rather, the intention is to establish the historical and social experience of life during these years while laying the groundwork for a materialist and historical interpretation of Baudelaire.

The three sections, "The Bohème," "The Flâneur," and "The Modern," are named for three subjects that recur within Baudelaire's writing. Instead of isolating these subjects, Benjamin presents an extensive network of material that establishes how pervasive each was within the social, political, and economic organization of this period.

The first section focuses on the bohème, and in particular on Marx's account of this figure as a professional conspirator whose life is defined by uncertainty and irregularity. By pursuing these qualities through the figures that populate the social sphere of the bohème, Benjamin establishes a group of associations that link poet and conspirator through a common denominator, the ragpicker. Benjamin writes:

> from the littérateur to the professional conspirator, everyone who belonged to the *bohème* could recognize a bit of himself in the ragpicker. Each person was in a more or less blunted state of revolt against society and faced a more or less precarious future. At the proper time, he was able to sympathize with those who were shaking the foundations of this society. The ragpicker was not alone in his dream.   (*SW* 4, 8)

After Benjamin asserts their common pursuit of what society leaves behind, he traces the affinity between the ragpicker and the poet right down to the physiology of Baudelaire:

> Ragpicker and poet: both are concerned with refuse, and both go about their solitary business while other citizens are sleeping; they even move in the same way. Nadar speaks of Baudelaire's "pas saccadé" [jerky gait].

> This is the gait of the poet who roams the city in search of rhyme-booty;
> it is also the gait of the ragpicker, who is obliged to come to a halt every
> few moments to gather up the refuse he encounters. There is much
> evidence indicating that Baudelaire secretly wished to develop this
> analogy.   (*SW* 4, 48)

Poet and ragpicker are both figures of isolation, experience exclusion, sympa-
thize with revolt, move in the world with a halting step, and find "the refuse of
society on their streets."

Given these shared conditions, modern existence for Benjamin's Baudelaire
requires a heroic attitude. In Benjamin's analysis, this attitude is an index to
the modern; however, it is an index that presents the modern as a force capable
of offering only death and suicide:

> The resistance that modernity offers to the natural productive élan of an
> individual is out of all proportion to his strength. It is understandable if
> a person becomes exhausted and takes refuge in death. Modernity must
> stand under the sign of suicide, an act which seals a heroic will that
> makes no concessions to a mentality inimical toward this will. Such a
> suicide is not resignation but heroic passion. It is *the* achievement of
> modernity in the realm of the passions.   (*SW* 4, 45)

In modernity the productive instinct is countered by an inability to sustain
itself. Like the poet's and ragpicker's gait, it falters. Contrary to expectation,
modernity is neither progress nor the overcoming of the past. Rather, its
achievement is found in downfall:

> [The poet] is destined for doom, no tragic poet need come forward to
> explain the conditions for this downfall. But once modernity has
> received its due, its time will have run out. Then it will be put to the test.
> After its end, it will be seen whether it itself will ever be able to become
> antiquity.   (*SW* 4, 49)

Tragic poets are no longer needed to explain the heroic figures of antiquity.
Modern heroes, Benjamin observes, can be found in the published records of
court proceedings. Not only do these heroes of the modern age lack conviction
but the heroic itself has become a role easily exchanged for another. For this
reason, Benjamin concludes his account of Baudelaire as the first "modern"
poet in the following terms:

> Because he did not have any convictions, he assumed ever new forms
> himself. Flâneur, apache, dandy, and ragpicker were so many roles to
> him. For the modern hero is no hero; he is a portrayer of heroes. Heroic

> modernity turns out to be a *Trauerspiel* in which the hero's part is
> available.   (*SW* 4, 60)

Dispersed and available to all, heroism becomes a commodity as modernity transforms even the ruins of the mourning play into something to be performed. If, in the *Trauerspiel* book, history has become the site of ruins, in the modern, the critical force Benjamin attaches to those ruins has been blunted in the nineteenth century by a commodification to which poet and ragpicker alike are not immune. The question posed by the modern in Benjamin's work is then a question of how to develop and sustain a critical analysis of social and economic forces whose grasp encompasses the ruins out of which the modern emerges in the Baroque.

Throughout "Paris of the Second Empire in Baudelaire," Benjamin's presentation of the bohemian, the flâneur, and the modern is so deeply embedded in historical association (even to the point of seeing the way Baudelaire walks as the effect of social and economic forces) that this essay threatens to disappear under the weight of its historical material. This aspect is precisely what Adorno questioned when he complained that the essay assembles rather than develops the motifs Benjamin has introduced from his work on the Arcades. Other remarks are harsher as Adorno tries to push the essay towards the theoretical analysis Benjamin withholds for the third and final part. At one point, Adorno asks, "is this material that can patiently wait for interpretation without being consumed by its own aura?" Above all, what the essay lacks for Adorno is a mediation of the "total process" at work in the economic, cultural, and political material Benjamin presents (see *C*, 580–81). In Benjamin's language, the "crystal of the total event" cannot be recognized.

It takes Benjamin a month to respond to Adorno's criticisms. His response asserts that Adorno has misread his treatment of the flâneur since that is "where theory comes into its own *without obstruction*" (*C*, 586). Already, this suggests that Benjamin responds to Adorno with a different understanding of theory. Where Adorno derives the theoretical from the mediation of the "total process," Benjamin locates theory in the manner of presentation. He writes, "this theory of the flâneur . . . fundamentally realizes a description of the flâneur I have had in mind for many years" (*C*, 586). Yet, despite this claim, it is not the flâneur who is meant to carry the theoretical weight of this essay. At this point in his development of this material, Benjamin emphasizes what he calls the "trace" as the one element to be given "sudden illumination" in the third, theoretical part of the book.

In his response to Adorno, Benjamin argues that his failure to develop the crucial role of the "trace" is the result of a "need to introduce [it] with complete impartiality at the empirical level." This need also informs the other sections of the essay and, together, they reflect his perception of the overall structure of this book: "the first part – Baudelaire as allegorist – poses the question; the third part presents the resolution. The second provides the requisite data for this resolution" (*C*, 574). The data Benjamin refers to include descriptions of the figure of the flâneur, Poe's invention of the detective story in the nineteenth century, the administrative organization of increasing aspects of daily life and existence, the emergence of the crowd and its narcotic effect as a defining characteristic of modern urban life, the intoxication of commodities, and Baudelaire's poetry. Through citations from fiction as well as historical accounts, Benjamin describes an urban existence in which experience is defined in the form of a trace that disappears into the crowd from which it has emerged. A central exhibit for this presentation is Baudelaire's poem "To a Woman Passing By," which focuses on the image of a woman the poet could have loved if the crowd had not let her appear and then vanish as a fleeting character only known by its disappearance. In this poem, contemporary experience becomes an experience of traces whose effect, Benjamin notes, is to provide a shock to the loneliness of the poet. Beyond this the trace remains undeveloped. The only clue to its eventual significance comes from Benjamin's response to Adorno when he claims that "the concept of trace will find its philosophical determination in opposition to the concept of aura" (*C*, 586). This remark underlines how central the trace is to Benjamin's thinking at this time, as well as his investment in articulating alternatives to the aesthetic history he has summarized under the name of the aura during the 1930s.

Despite Benjamin's claim that the second section of the essay contains a theory of the flâneur (*C*, 586), this theory does not develop the kind of critique of commodity fetish and its means of production that Adorno has in mind. However, it does possess a degree of mediation of the "total process" to the extent that Benjamin links the flâneur to the process of commodification that emerges with the phantasmagorical in the nineteenth century. Of this figure, Benjamin writes:

> The flâneur is someone abandoned in the crowd. He is thus in the same situation as the commodity. He is unaware of this special situation, but this does not diminish its effect on him; it permeates him blissfully, like a narcotic that can compensate him for many humiliations. The intoxication to which the flâneur surrenders is the intoxication of the commodity immersed in a surging stream of customers.   (*SW* 4, 31)

Benjamin's presentation of the flâneur is deeply embedded in his account of both the phantasmagorical character of the nineteenth century and his perception of an intoxication that not only runs through the nineteenth century but also persists in the twentieth century within surrealism. To awake from this intoxication or dream-like state is a goal that the Baudelaire writings share with *The Arcades Project*. Both aim to produce an account of history and culture that also participates in a revolutionary politics. Although Benjamin connects this type of politics to the flâneur through an analysis of the commodity fetish, no such connection is evident for the trace. Benjamin's need to document commodification and the aura it casts around objects, culture, and social organization leaves little room to unfold the significance he places on his concept of the trace. Since the intent is always to reserve such a development for the final part, Benjamin's essay already confronts us with the question posed by the form in which the materials belonging to *The Arcades Project* have survived. While Benjamin's letters and the fragments associated with his work on Baudelaire promise an answer to this question, it is also clear that the resolution Benjamin sought still remained to be fully developed.

(ii) "On Some Motifs in Baudelaire" (February–July 1939)

A star without atmosphere.

Adorno's unwillingness to accept "Paris of the Second Empire in Baudelaire" for publication led Benjamin to propose focusing on the theory of the flâneur as its focal point while giving a more central role to the critique of the masses (*C*, 589). With this focus in mind Benjamin began work on the revision in February 1939 and, by the end of July, produced the essay that was published in January 1940 as "On Some Motifs in Baudelaire." This rewrite of "The Flâneur" produces an essay with a quite different emphasis from the 1938 version. Foremost is the place Benjamin gives to the experience of shock. Shock had a limited role in the first essay where it was presented as the experience the poet feels after being struck by the image of a woman in the crowd. There, the source of the shock is not located in this woman's image but rather in the poet's loneliness. Now, in "On Some Motifs" Benjamin will assert that "Baudelaire placed shock experience (*Chockerfahrung*) at the very center of his art" (*SW* 4, 319). Also, although the translation does not catch this, the shock Benjamin builds this essay around involves the distinction between the two kinds of experience presented in "The Storyteller" in 1936: the experience of daily life (*Erlebnis*) and the experience that develops across history and time (*Erfahrung*). In the sentence just cited, shock belongs to the longer kind of experience (*Chockerfahrung*). However, this does not mean that shock is always associated with that form of experience. Later in this essay, when Benjamin discusses the crowd he equates shock with the short-lived kind of experience described by *Erlebnis*. The relation between these two kinds of shock experience provides the central thread with which Benjamin makes his way through observations on Baudelaire, the flâneur, the crowd, and, borrowing a topic from the essay on technical reproducibility, the crisis of artistic reproduction.

Benjamin begins this essay with general reflections on the reception and significance of lyric poetry which link changes in its reception to changes in the structure of experience. After noting how nineteenth-century attempts to define true experience remain untouched by historical conditions, Benjamin turns to what Proust termed *mémoire involontaire* (see earlier discussion of Benjamin's Proust essay) in order to introduce the question pursued in this essay. The question is, how is long experience possible within a modernity that has witnessed the weakening of experience into isolated moments? The significance of this question for Benjamin's work is immense, since without some means of linking the modern to long experience, analysis of the historical meaning of the modern becomes impossible. In this respect, what is at stake in this essay is the attempt to establish the historical understanding of an age in which historical meaning and daily experience seem to have little relation to one another.

While Proust provides one example of how this relation is explored, Freud provides Benjamin with a "more substantial definition" (*SW* 4, 316). The turn to Freud marks a considerable change from the first essay as Benjamin seeks to provide a stronger basis for the two kinds of experience presented in this essay. In Freud, Benjamin finds a discussion of consciousness and memory that he can align with isolated and long experience. Since consciousness deals with events as they happen, it is concerned with *Erlebnis*, or isolated experience. Memory, on the other hand, deals with long experience. Citing Freud, Benjamin observes that consciousness and memory are so different from one another that they are "incompatible processes." However, again following Freud, Benjamin notes that they operate "within one and the same system" (*SW* 4, 317). This system involves the way in which consciousness operates as a defense against "excessive energies at work in the external world." In Freud, consciousness restricts the effect of these energies so that they remain isolated experiences. Consciousness, in this case, is a means of dealing with a threat. Benjamin summarizes: "The threat posed by these energies is the threat of shocks. The more readily consciousness registers these shocks, the less likely they are to have a traumatic effect" (*SW* 4, 317).

To the extent that consciousness can parry or cushion the shocks of daily or isolated experiences, it blocks the supply of material that poetry acts upon in order to produce long experience. Thus, Benjamin asks: "One wonders how lyric poetry can be grounded in experience (*Erfahrung*) when exposure to shock (*Chockerlebnis*) has become the norm" (*SW* 4, 318). Despite this question, Baudelaire becomes the pre-eminent modern poet for Benjamin – precisely because he registers the experience of modern life in a poetry that seeks "emancipation from isolated experiences" (*SW* 4, 318). This does not mean that emancipation is easily achieved or obtained at no cost. The process, Benjamin notes, is described by Baudelaire in terms of fear: "He speaks of a duel in which the artist, just before being beaten, screams in fright. This duel is the creative process itself" (*SW* 4, 319). The scream registers the failure of consciousness to cushion the blow the poet is about to receive. In this way, shock bypasses the efforts of consciousness to restrict and isolate it. Instead, it is registered traumatically. Consequently, this defining aspect of modern experience becomes available to the poetic process as something other than an isolated experience.

Benjamin sees the rescue of long experience as the mission of Baudelaire's poetry. This mission is not, however, undertaken with the kind of self-deception that fosters blind faith in its achievement. What Benjamin terms Baudelaire's "heroism" stems precisely from the fact that the poet takes on such a mission while recognizing, that he must do so with "the impotent rage of someone fighting the rain or the wind" (*SW* 4, 343). Given this recognition, long experience should not be viewed as something that can be sustained easily within modernity. For one thing, the nature of modern experience, as exemplified by the crowd, constantly works against it. For another, the poet's role as the communicator of the kind of long experience Benjamin describes in "The Storyteller" can no longer be taken for granted. The poet is fated to struggle against the crowd that defines the modern in order to wrest "the weight of long experience" from the isolated experience it constantly presents. As the conclusion to this essay indicates, the significance of Baudelaire's poetry resides, for Benjamin, in this struggle with the forces that define his age:

> He named the price for which the sensation of modernity could be had: the disintegration of the aura in immediate shock experience [*Chockerlebnis*]. He paid dearly for consenting to this disintegration – but it is the law of his poetry. This poetry appears in the sky of the Second Empire as "a star without atmosphere." (*SW* 4, 343)

This last image, borrowed from Nietzsche, confirms the law of a poetry condemned by its own mission to rescue long experience. Baudelaire's poetry could only shine as a star in the sky to the extent that it registered the presence of the forces against which it fought but from which it could draw no atmosphere to sustain itself – unlike the auratic art of the past. Benjamin's Baudelaire thus enters the orbit of a modernity from which the political, cultural, and economic significance of the present is perceived through the disintegration of the past. In this aspect, the projected Baudelaire book, as Benjamin indicated, attempts to accomplish for the nineteenth century what his study of the mourning play did for the Baroque. But he does so by pushing that earlier book's understanding of history towards an account of modernity as an age fated to rescue its own ruin from the ruins of contemporary, isolated experience.

Suggested further reading

Andrew Benjamin. "Tradition and Experience: Walter Benjamin's 'On Some
   Motifs in Baudelaire.'" In his *The Problems of Modernity: Adorno and
   Benjamin*. London: Routledge, 1989. 122–40.
Michael W. Jennings. "Benjamin's Baudelaire: The Shape of Benjamin's Mature
   Criticism." In his *Dialectical Images: Walter Benjamin's Theory of
   Literary Criticism*. Ithaca: Cornell University Press, 1987. 15–41.
Rainer Nägele. "The Poetic Ground Laid Bare (Benjamin Reading Baudelaire)."
   In *Walter Benjamin: Theoretical Questions*. Ed. David S. Ferris. Stanford:
   Stanford University Press, 1996. 118–38.

"On the Concept of History" (1939–1940)

> A unique experience with the past.

In a letter to Adorno written in May 1940, Benjamin emphasizes the relation between this work and his studies of Baudelaire: "[the theses] present a certain stage of my reflections in continuation of the Baudelaire" (*C*, 630). Written after the completion of "On Some Motifs in Baudelaire," the theses provide a condensed account of the historical questions posed by both *The Arcades Project* and the study of Baudelaire. But, like these major projects, "On the Concept of History" remains a work in progress at the time of his death in September 1940.

The importance of this work cannot be underestimated both within the immediate context of his thought in the late 1930s and within the greater trajectory of his career. A concern with history and the articulation of its significance in the present can be traced from Benjamin's early writings, including those that predate his exposure to Lukács and Marxism in 1924. In April 1940, in a letter to Adorno's wife Gretel, Benjamin describes the long presence of history in his thinking while also noting the occasion of this work: "The war and the constellation it brought with it has led me to set down certain thoughts about which I can say that I have held them safe with myself for almost twenty years, yes, even from myself" (*GB* 6, 435). In this context, he goes on to draw special attention to Thesis XVII as the one that "would have to reveal the hidden but conclusive relationship between these observations and my previous works" (*GB* 6, 436).

Topics expressed in Thesis XVII are readily recognizable in Benjamin's writings: the emphasis on the constructive, on the double sense of thinking as a movement and the arrest of that movement, on constellation, on historical materialism, and on an aspect that has always been present but which comes strongly to the fore again, the messianic. All these aspects of Benjamin's thought are now enlisted in a method whose intention is "to blast a specific era out of the homogeneous course of history" (*SW* 4, 396). Despite the image of "blasting," this is not a destructive undertaking but rather a restructuring of history that seeks to preserve the objects it attends to while allowing the emergence of what has been oppressed in the past. When Benjamin describes this method at the end of Thesis XVII, the blueprint for his Baudelaire book is easily discerned: "As a result of this method, the lifework is both preserved and sublated *in* the work, the era *in* the lifework, and the entire course of history *in* the era" (*SW* 4, 396). This remark makes clear just how expansive Benjamin's treatment of history has become. What is now at stake – and in a situation that can only magnify this sense – is the entire course of history. Here, the task confronting Benjamin is to find a means of articulating this history without collapsing under the weight of accumulated historical material – which is precisely what he sees happening within traditional accounts that seek to ascribe a universal significance to history in the form of progress. Against such accounts, this work seeks a "theoretical armature" in order to avoid a method whose procedure simply "musters a mass of data to fill the homogeneous empty time" (*SW* 4, 396). With this goal in mind, Benjamin's struggle with the material he has gathered for *The Arcades Project* is brought to a crucial focus in such an "armature," thereby making this work an important statement on the significance of that project.

One of the distinctive aspects of Benjamin's account of history in this late work is the role he gives to the messianic in relation to the historical materialism that had defined his work on Baudelaire and *The Arcades Project*. Thesis XVII summarizes this relation as follows:

> The historical materialist approaches a historical object only where it confronts him as a monad. In this structure he recognizes the sign of a messianic arrest of happening, or (to put it differently) a revolutionary chance in the fight for the oppressed past.   (*SW* 4, 396)

Whenever a historical object appears as a monad, that is, whenever it is separated from the continuous flow of events and objects through time, there occurs the messianic arrest in which history is brought to a standstill. In this arrest, Benjamin sees the possibility of recognizing a past no longer oppressed by the ideologies that have determined not just historical study but the understanding of what history itself is (for example, the view that the task of history is simply to know the past "the way it really was" [*SW* 4, 391]). Although Benjamin presents his approach in revolutionary terms, he does not consider revolution to be a foregone conclusion. He only speaks of "a revolutionary chance." By referring to the "messianic arrest of happening" as the opening of such a chance, Benjamin underlines the precariousness of the historical position he describes in this work. Grasping this precariousness is essential in order to understand Benjamin's concept of history in this his last work.

In Thesis V, precariousness plays a crucial role when Benjamin describes how "the true image of the past" appears. He writes that "The past can only be seized as an image that flashes up at the moment of its recognizability and is never seen again" (*SW* 4, 390). Two important aspects of Benjamin's historical thinking are stated here: the past can only be recognized in an image and this recognition occurs in a specific moment, the present that offers "a unique experience with the past" (Thesis XVI; *SW* 4, 396). Benjamin opposes this unique experience to the kind of history he calls "historicism" – where the present is only understood as a transition. The present in Benjamin is an interruptive force. However, its power of interruption is short-lived. The image of the past that flashes up in the present "flits by." But what is crucial in this "flitting by" is that the present still recognizes itself as "intended in that image" (*SW* 4, 391). "Intended" means that the significance of the past which has been recognized can only be recognized in this specific present moment. Here, the unique experience at the heart of this concept of history emerges: when the present recognizes itself as intended it also realizes its historical significance as the moment that arrests the historical illusions present in ideas such as progress and so on. This recognition makes the present stand out from the course of history since it is the one place where history occurs in a meaningful way – that is, in a way that allows the appearance of the revolutionary potential concealed in the ideologies of the past. Only the present is capable of recognizing this potential and only this recognition has any meaning for the present.

Although Benjamin recognizes such potential in this "true image of the past," he also adds two conditions that complicate its ability to change the political and historical situation in which it occurs. The first has already been mentioned: the image does not stay put, it flits by. The second condition states that this image "unexpectedly appears to the historical subject in a moment of danger" (*SW* 4, 391). Benjamin glosses this danger as something that "threatens both the content of the tradition and those who inherit it. For both, it is one and the same thing: the danger of becoming a tool of the ruling classes" (*SW* 4, 391). The past, here called tradition, is always in danger of being appropriated for political purposes. Benjamin tries to resist this appropriation through an image that does not already participate in a process whose outcome is pre-determined – as is the case with the idea of progress or the political goals of fascism. The revolutionary potential of Benjamin's historical image is located here; it interrupts such ideas and goals. However, its ability to interrupt is not accompanied by an ability to resist either progress or fascism. Despite the interruptive, critical power this image exerts, Benjamin tells us that there is a "conformism . . . working to overpower it" (*SW* 4, 391). The image that "flits by" and is "never seen again" does not endure in the face of the forces lined up against it.

Despite this danger, Benjamin maintains the hope that history possesses something that will redeem it; however, this hope is by no means uncondi-tional: "The only historian capable of fanning the spark of hope in the past is the one who is firmly convinced that *even the dead* will not be safe from the enemy if he is victorious. And this enemy has never ceased to be victorious" (*SW* 4, 391). Neither the past nor the dead are safe from an enemy whose victories give it the right to determine the past and what it means. This power-lessness lies behind a much cited sentence from this work, namely, "there is no document of culture which is not at the same time a document of barbarism" (*SW* 4, 392). This sentence indicates both the weakness of culture when con-fronted by the barbaric enemy and the precariousness of the critical position Benjamin develops here. To articulate a historical understanding that does not end up repeating historicism, this understanding cannot rely on victory for its justification. This is why Benjamin makes the true image of the past something fleeting that can never be repeated. Its critical effect arises from the counter-weight this precariousness offers to the ideological illusions of historicism such as progress, universal history and, ultimately, fascism. However, the price paid for this critical effect is the inability of Benjamin's "true image of the past" to stand in an enduring way against the forces of conformism. As a result, its real significance lies in its ability to illuminate those forces and, in this way, open up the chance of a revolutionary outcome.

This understanding of history reveals the strongly messianic character of Benjamin's historical thinking. Although the messianic has been an element in Benjamin's thinking for a long time – already in his first dissertation, he speaks of the messianic element in German Romanticism – it emerges here as a crucial component. It is first referred to in Thesis II when Benjamin explains how "the past carries with it a secret index by which it is referred to redemption." This index is subsequently defined as "a secret agreement between past generations and the present one" (*SW* 4, 390). This agreement takes the form of a claim that the past makes on a power that the present possesses. This power, Benjamin states, is messianic but a weak messianic power. It is weak because it cannot proclaim the end of history – only the arrival of the Messiah can do this. Yet, like the Messiah, this power has the ability to arrest the flow of time. Here, the difference between the messianic and the Messiah is that the former can only arrest time in the form of an interruption. However, in that interruption (which is when the "true image of the past" occurs), history is redeemed from the ideological forces that have distorted it. The possibility of redeeming the past from the "forces of conformism" rests on this power. Without it, the secret index or agreement between the past and the present cannot take place.

For Benjamin, historical materialism's ability to bring time to a standstill in an image is in step with the weak messianic power that informs his concept of history. This does not mean that Benjamin's thinking and writing conclude with a theological concept of history. A theological conclusion would demand the arrival of the Messiah. This is where the importance of Benjamin's emphasis on the messianic or what is *like* the Messiah is crucial. What Benjamin offers is a messianic concept of history into which no Messiah steps. What appears through his historical materialism are only "models" or "tremendous abbreviations" of what the Messiah offers. Accordingly, the task of the historical materialist is to establish "a concept of the present as the now-time in which splinters of messianic time are interspersed" (*SW* 4, 397). Accordingly, the Messiah does not appear. Only the messianic is present and only then in a fragmentary form. With this distinction, Benjamin refuses a theological solution to a history because it would have neither political nor historical meaning. Where redemption of the past occurs, it must occur within history in order to have political significance. But, in this case, the redemption offered by the messianic, as Benjamin indicates in a fragmentary text from 1938–39, is a "small fissure in the continuous catastrophe" ("Central Park," *SW* 4, 185). The rescue of this small fissure from a history that threatens to overpower it at every moment forms the basis of Benjamin's concept of history. Historical materialism is adopted here as a method precisely because the messianic power lodged in this fissure is weak; it cannot defeat what threatens it. This fissure, this splinter of messianic time is, for Benjamin, the revolutionary chance that no other concept of history appears able to offer.

Suggested further reading

Howard Caygill. "Non-Messianic Political Theology in Benjamin's 'On the Concept of History.'" In *Walter Benjamin and History*. Ed. Andrew Benjamin. London: Continuum Books, 2005. 215–26.

Michael Löwy. *Fire Alarm: Reading Walter Benjamin's* "On the Concept of History." London: Verso, 2006.

Irving Wohlfarth. "On the Messianic Structure of Walter Benjamin's Last Reflections," *Glyph* 3. Baltimore: Johns Hopkins University Press, 1978. 148–212.

Critical reception

Today, Walter Benjamin is far from succumbing to the fate of the Russian Jewish philosopher whose widow he describes in 1939 as sitting alone in her Paris apartment surrounded by uncut volumes of her husband's works (*C*, 594). This was not always the case. From the time of his death in 1940 to the mid-1960s, a relatively small part of his total output was available, and only then in German. But what did become available in these years played a significant role in shaping Benjamin's subsequent reception and influence. Now, fifty years after the initial post-war publication of his essays, Benjamin's renown is such that he has spawned an immense amount of secondary writing about his critical and cultural analyses. Four phases can be distinguished in this reception: an initial stage beginning in the 1950s as Benjamin's writings begin to be published in Germany; a second phase in which Benjamin's Marxism and later association with the Frankfurt School is prominent; a third phase in which the theoretical and critical character of much of his writing is emphasized as literary theory comes to the fore; a fourth phase in which he gains an ever wider reception within the disparate disciplines of the humanities and the social sciences.

Translation and early history of reception

This first phase can be traced to the publication of a two-volume edition of Benjamin's writings by Theodor Adorno in 1955. This edition is followed by another two-volume edition (the first of which was published as *Illuminationen* in 1961 and the second as *Angelus Novus* in 1966). Along with several shorter volumes, these publications provided the basic texts through which Benjamin would be introduced into the English-speaking world.

Benjamin's introduction in English began in 1968 with the publication of *Illuminations*, edited by Hannah Arendt. Although it takes its name from the 1961 German edition, this volume contains approximately half of the essays published in that earlier edition. Other translations followed in the 1970s: *Understanding Brecht* (1973); *Charles Baudelaire: A Lyric Poet in the Era of High Capitalism* (1973); *Origin of German Tragic Drama* (1977); *Reflections: Essays, Aphorisms, Autobiographical Writings* (1978); *One-Way Street, and Other Writings* (1979). None of these volumes challenged the place of Arendt's volume as the most widely read edition of Benjamin's essays in English. However, what is remarkable about this sequence of volumes in the 1970s is that all but one appeared from the London publisher New Left Books – itself an indication of the context in which Benjamin was initially received.

The second phase began with the publication between 1971 and 1989 of the German collected edition of Benjamin's writings. The effect of this edition on his reception can be easily gauged from the size of this publication, which runs to almost 8,000 pages including editorial notes and commentary. In comparison to what Benjamin published during his lifetime, his collected works established an extensive *œuvre* that presents not just the already published writings but also many previously unknown materials and many manuscripts and revisions that help trace the development of his thought.

An immediate effect of the editorial work for the German edition was to provide a broader context in which to set the already known materials. Perhaps most importantly, it allowed the massive project to which Benjamin devoted thirteen years of his life, *The Arcades Project*, to emerge from the shadows and assume a concrete, albeit fragmentary, form in which it could at least be studied. This collected edition set the stage for a more exhaustive edition of Benjamin's works in English. Between 1996 and 2003, the four-volume *Selected Writings* appeared from Harvard University Press. This publication made just over 2,200 pages of Benjamin's writings available in English, many of which appear in English for the first time. While this edition has become the standard reference in English, it is still by no means as complete as the German edition. However, its range presents a picture of his work that is broader than the one available from the many individual volumes previously available. By itself, this breadth demands a more comprehensive reception for Benjamin's writings as well as a more comprehensive account of his development, including the intellectual currents that run through his work.

In addition to the textual history that provides the basis for Benjamin's reception, there is also the interpretative reception. In some respects, the interpretative reception is difficult to separate from this history. From early on, the publication of Benjamin's writings tended to cultivate the very thing that he spent many of his last years trying to dispel: an aura. In the case of Benjamin, this aura has been fueled by a tragic death and the massive promise of his last projects. Add to this a body of writing that invokes many areas of interest and it is easy to see how easily Benjamin became not only a desirable figure to invoke but also a figure who could reflect many of the critical desires projected on to him. Unresolved issues in his own work, for instance the strong pull of theological and Marxist tendencies, prompted attempts to reclaim his work in the name of one or the other. Adorno most clearly pursued the latter and in so doing sought to bring Benjamin more firmly into the circle of the Frankfurt School and its practice of critical theory. Scholem, particularly in his memoir *The Story of a Friendship*, discounts Benjamin's Marxist commitments and claims significance for his theological and Jewish side. In their own ways, both sought to establish a picture of Benjamin free from the influence of Brecht. If these were the stakes in the early reception of Benjamin, the picture changed dramatically as Benjamin was introduced through translation into a wider context.

While Adorno's account of Benjamin emphasized the philosophical aspect of his thinking – an emphasis that would dominate his reception in Germany for years to come – and Scholem emphasized his theological leanings, a whole aspect of his writings was eclipsed. This aspect is stressed by Hannah Arendt when she states that the intention of the first volume of his writings in English, *Illuminations*, was to establish "the importance of Benjamin as a literary critic" (*Illuminations*, 264). Clearly, Benjamin's Marxist leanings would not be the best calling card for a critic being introduced in a volume first published in New York barely ten years after the heyday of McCarthyism and even less after the height of the Cold War. Yet, this political consideration risks concealing the single most important factor in determining Benjamin's reception after the late 1960s: the exponential growth in critical and theoretical interests within the modern university. As before, in the 1950s, this reception took the form of claims upon Benjamin that were focused on a restricted selection of his works, if not on one in particular: "The Work of Art in the Age of Its Technical Reproducibility." At the same time, the irony that this reception was driven by the kind of institution that had rejected him in 1925 should not be missed. The unfolding of this reception does, however, pose the question of whether Benjamin's work had finally realized the time and context in which it could be recognized or whether his work had just made a leap from mere misunderstanding by the academy to what he called "enthusiastic misunderstandings" in a late letter to Gretel Adorno.

Benjamin's reception has proceeded along several different lines of development. There are distinct national differences. His German reception, and to a large degree his French reception, has been more philosophical than in other countries. In contrast, his Spanish reception, like his initial introduction into English, emphasized his role as a literary critic. However, none of these national contexts experienced to the same degree the diffusion of his writings into as broad a collection of disciplines and contexts as his recent reception in the English-speaking world. A sign of this diffusion is the regularity with which his work is now regularly taught and referred to in media studies, art history, film studies, cultural studies, architecture, photography, literature, and literary and cultural theory, and also in relation to continental philosophy – to name the most prominent.

Despite Benjamin's diffusion into so many different areas, it is possible to discern three main concentrations according to which his reception into late twentieth-century criticism has taken place. First, there is the left-wing reception which picks up on his relation to the Frankfurt School; second, literary theory; third, cultural criticism and cultural history. In broader terms, these three areas may be described as political and Marxist, philosophical and theoretical, and historical and material. The fact that these three areas were never quite separate in Benjamin's later writings indicates the extent to which his reception is engaged in the attempt to define his significance by emphasizing one aspect or another of his work. Also to be considered is the part played by different critical discourses in his reception since it is possible to identify each of these areas with one discourse or another. While Benjamin's reception mirrors the relation between these discourses and their institutional history, what is equally at work is a desire to claim legitimacy either from his writings or from their revisionary interpretation. Thus, two approaches that Benjamin did not separate, Marxism and materialism, will find themselves distinguished as cultural criticism pursues its emphasis on material objects but without Benjamin's explicitly revolutionary and Marxist inflection. It is as if the theological element that the left-wing reception dances around is to be repeated, except in this case his Marxism is being de-emphasized. Such a Benjamin is being rescued for a context in which adherence to the Marxist and the theological elements of his work cannot be given overt significance.

In many ways, Benjamin's reception is a reflection of both the recent history of critical schools and the difficulty of assigning him a definitive place within that history. As a result, it is easier to address his reception by identifying the three general phases according to which it has occurred, while bearing in mind that these phases also reflect emphases that have significant historical overlap.

Political and Marxist-influenced reception

The early publication history of Benjamin in English already signals how his work was perceived within left-wing politics. Between 1973 and 1979, four volumes appear from New Left Books. Furthermore, one of the earliest essays on Benjamin to appear in English is published in 1970 by Fredric Jameson whose own work is well known for its roots in Marxist criticism. This essay, reprinted in Jameson's 1971 book, *Marxism and Form*, presents Benjamin as someone whose movement from aesthetic to political and historical concerns is brought about by history itself – thereby affirming the Marxist thesis that meaning (in this case, Benjamin's meaning) is socially and historically determined. That Benjamin should be fitted to this interpretation is easy to understand. His later works almost seem to demand it. But how does one reconcile Benjamin's Marxist tendencies on the one hand, and, on the other, his obsessive interest in children's toys and books? Or, to cite the more familiar issue, Benjamin's pairing of the theological (in the form of the messianic) with Marxism? This second issue causes some discomfort since theology is precisely the kind of ideology that materialist and Marxist criticism unmasks. In a later book, Jameson deals with this by asserting that the theological is "strategic" in Benjamin (*Political Unconscious*, 69n). Jameson is not the only critic who registers this question within the leftist reception of Benjamin. Terry Eagleton, in *Walter Benjamin or Towards a Revolutionary Criticism* (1981), also has to deal with the question of how to rescue a revolutionary criticism from Benjamin – which amounts to rescuing it from the critic responsible for introducing it in the first place. This task leads Eagleton to emphasize a contradiction between idealism and Marxism in Benjamin. The result of this emphasis is a picture of Benjamin as a figure whose work dramatizes the need for the revolutionary criticism on which he pinned so much hope. Eagleton's account of Benjamin becomes symptomatic of the difficulties that Marxist criticism faces in general: how to sustain a politically based critical project in an age radically different from the historical age from which Marxism emerged. Benjamin also faced this difficulty in his later work. When this difficulty is repeated in his reception, it is clear that the critical questions Benjamin reflected and confronted are not easily overcome by calling one side of his work idealist and the other political or materialistic. In a curious twist, Eagleton's commitment to a radical, historical, and materialist criticism re-enacts Benjamin's position. The difficulty this reception has in dealing with Benjamin's messianic Marxism is striking if only because it does not ask whether Benjamin's use of the messianic is a response to an inadequacy within Marxism rather than the simpler intrusion of a theologically tinged ideology. Within this reception, the question of Benjamin's

Marxism may always remain unresolved, and precisely because of the extent to which Benjamin's work has never been completely assimilated to a political orthodoxy whether Marxist or neo-Marxist.

Reception in literary and critical theory

If the determination of Benjamin's Marxism dominated the early phase of his reception – into at least the early 1980s – the subsequent phase showed a greater inclination to deal with what Habermas, in 1972, termed a body of work "disposed to a history of disparate effects."[1] In this phase, Benjamin began to emerge more strongly as a cultural theoretician as his writings were taken up in a wider range of disciplines within university departments in the US and the UK: literary, film studies, art history, and continental philosophy, to name those that were among the first to do so. Specific issues from different points of his career received attention. Book-length studies of his work as a whole began to appear (Roberts 1982; Wolin 1982; Gilloch 2002) as well as books on some of his central concerns: modernity (Nägele 1991); literary criticism (Jennings 1987); the arcades (Buck-Morss 1989); allegory and dialectics (Pensky 1993); tradition (McCole 1993); surrealism (Cohen 1993); city (Gilloch 1996); history (Steinberg 1996; Hanssen 1998); photography (Cadava 1997); experience (Caygill 1998); autobiography (Richter 2000). Beside these books focused singly on Benjamin, other studies have placed his thought within the context of contemporaries or more general critical issues (see John Frisby, *Fragments of Modernity*; Susan Handelman, *Fragments of Redemption*; and Andrew Benjamin, *Style and Time*). In addition, there has been a steady tide of edited volumes on both general and focused topics as well as special issues by journals, most notably in *New German Critique, Diacritics,* and *Critical Inquiry*. Add to this the immense number of essays published on Benjamin since 1980.

This sampling of work from the US and the UK underlines not only the disparate reception of Benjamin from 1980 on, but also how much this reception occurred through authors whose careers were based in literary study. The more philosophical emphasis of his German reception has not been entirely missing though. Rather, it took a different turn, one that happened to coincide with the rise of literary theory and deconstruction. Work belonging to this area of reception is strongly represented by Andrew Benjamin, Rodolphe Gasché, Werner Hamacher, and Samuel Weber – not to mention Jacques Derrida and Paul de Man. Here, the question of the extent to which Benjamin can be appropriated to a contemporary critical approach (as well as the question of the extent to which Benjamin anticipates this approach) comes to the fore in a way that recalls the debate concerning his relation to Marxism. An essay such as Anselm Haverkamp's "Notes on the Dialectical Image (How Deconstructive Is It?)" reflects these questions.[2] Yet, it is clear that deconstruction found a considerable affinity in Benjamin. Two long works by Derrida are devoted to essays that have had considerable resonance within deconstructive criticism: Benjamin's "Critique of Violence" and "The Task of the Translator." Derrida's reading of the first is far from programmatic in the sense that Benjamin's writing and thinking is recovered as a prototype. Derrida remarks: "this text, in all its polysemic mobility and all its resources for reversal, seems to me finally to resemble too closely, to the point of specular fascination and vertigo, the very thing against which one must act and think, do and speak."[3] This reservation recognizes the difference between Benjamin's analysis and a more contemporary reflection on the issues confronted by that analysis. More than the "Critique of Violence," Benjamin's essay on translation has had an important place in the rapprochement of Benjamin and deconstructive criticism. In addition to Derrida, Paul de Man and Carol Jacobs have written on this essay in a way that highlights both Benjamin's untranslatability and the untranslatability he places at the center of his discussion. What emerges from their readings of Benjamin's essay is an engagement with the issues criticism faces when confronting the language of a text – issues that each sees codified in Benjamin's reflection on translation.

In addition to this focus on translation, Benjamin's development of allegory also had a significant place at this stage of his reception. Its influence is particularly marked in the evolution of Paul de Man's theoretical writings. The influence of Benjamin's treatment of allegory is, however, broader than this deconstructive context. Allegory also figured importantly in his Marxist reception: Jameson defines it within his own understanding of history while Eagleton places it firmly within a Marxist analysis as a commodity. The broad reception of allegory indicates how much is at stake in accommodating this key concept, lest the ruins it produced in the Baroque drama are visited upon Benjamin's interpreters. Yet, in the end, Benjamin's theoretical reception has done more to rescue allegory for modern criticism than any other concept in his writings, excepting aura. Rather than neutralize allegory, this reception has emphasized the problematic relation of language to meaning at work in this mode of presentation. The emphasis on language, while perhaps expected in a theoretical-deconstructive context, has also been studied significantly in books such as Peter Fenves's *Arresting Language* (2001) – a book that contributes greatly to an understanding of philosophical and intellectual traditions within which Benjamin's reflection and language take place. This broadening of the theoretical and philosophical framework within which Benjamin is studied is also present across the work of Samuel Weber who, in addition to essays on various questions posed by Benjamin, has explored his writings in the context of modern media (*Mass Mediauras*, 2001) and the institutionalization of modern criticism and literary study. These developments signal above all else that the textual and language questions explored within this reception have evolved into areas concerned with violence, law, politics, dialectics, media, and the place of the image in contemporary experience.

Benjamin across disciplines and in recent critical approaches

Despite the currency given to Benjamin by the turn towards theory in the late 1970s and 1980s, the turn away from theoretical study did not slow Benjamin's rising importance as the foremost literary and cultural critic of the twentieth century. In many respects, the more theoretical phase of his development solidified his modern critical position not only within literary study but more broadly across the humanities and into the social sciences. Not coincidentally, this phase of his reception has coincided with the reinvention of some disciplines such as art history, as well as with the emergence of more materially focused types of criticism such as cultural studies.

Benjamin's analysis of photography and the auratic gave art history the basis for a radical change in its methods and practices. In contrast to art history's long-standing focus on the appreciation of style and its development across historical periods, Benjamin provided an alternative source for its significance by emphasizing the functional role that art plays in history. His concept of the aura also provided a means of demarcating the ways in which a traditional and canonical history of art can be questioned through a transformation of what history means in relation to art. Benjamin's materialist studies in *The Arcades Project* have also had an impact in this field's approach to what it can and should study. Prompted by Benjamin's example, art history fostered a broader study of visual material under the name of visual culture. This view of the visual world is summarized by Jules David Prown as "all artifacts, all objects made or modified by human agency." Thus, visual culture becomes a "cultural art history" that investigates "the entire range of visual and material culture."[4] Benjamin's omnivorous research into the social and cultural history of nineteenth-century Paris is clearly an early model for this development. But this is not the only area in which the contemporary study of art has turned to Benjamin. The changing media of art have also provided a welcome to Benjamin's ideas on technology, particularly with the appearance of digital and video art. But what is at stake here is far from Benjamin's optimism that his concepts would be useless to fascism. Instead, it is a means to interpret the significance of art forms not accessible to the vocabulary and methods developed for traditional art. Through this reception in art history, there is a sense that Benjamin's "hour of full satisfaction has come," even if it is not the satisfaction nor the context Benjamin had in mind when he wrote this phrase.

Like art history, and like the early Marxist phase of Benjamin's reception, the discipline of cultural studies has shown greater openness to his later work. For this reason, it is not surprising that the emphasis of cultural studies on the social and political codes operating through objects of mass consumption should turn to *The Arcades Project* as its central Benjaminian exhibit. This focus is abundantly clear in Angela McRobbie's 1993 essay, "The Place of Walter Benjamin in Cultural Studies" (published in *The Cultural Studies Reader*, a manifesto in all but name for this approach). Yet, McRobbie's claim to rescue Benjamin's later work for cultural studies is based largely on the account of *The Arcades Project* mediated through Susan Buck-Morss's reconstruction in *The Dialectics of Seeing*. Benjamin's work was not available in English at this point. Despite the obvious point of contact between cultural studies and Benjamin's analyses of commodification and mass consumption, there are important differences in method and approach which became more obvious once *The Arcades Project* appeared in translation in 1999. It is as if the idea of Benjamin's project offers a promise to this approach that far exceeds its actual existence as a fragmented text with more historical than methodological significance. Is this why, when the editor of *The Cultural Studies Reader*, Simon During, publishes *Cultural Studies: A Critical Introduction* in 2005, Benjamin has no place in either the text or its bibliography despite shared intentions?

If Benjamin's role as either theoretician or practitioner of cultural studies is less prominent, the same cannot be said about his significance for the field of media studies and its focus on the study of contemporary technological culture. In the work of Douglas Kellner (see his *Media Studies*, 1995), media studies shares an affinity with the Marxist emphasis of Jameson and Eagleton. Like them, Kellner recognizes the interaction of text and historical forces as a basis for developing social critique. However, the focus of this field is directed towards the synthesis of technology, ideology, and knowledge that occurs within modern media. Yet, this emphasis on social and ideological criticism is not the only way in which the influence of Benjamin can be discerned in media studies. Other analyses of form in media have explored the structure of television genres (for instance, daytime television's use of the interruptive technique Benjamin sees as the basis of cinematic experience). This example indicates a generalizing tendency that also occurred with Benjamin's reception in film studies. This tendency can be discerned in the way that film studies took up Benjamin as a crucial theoretical frame at an early stage of its development. The theoretical insight Benjamin offered helped propel his single essay on film to a height that allowed it to stand beside and even eclipse the more extensive but equally important work of his friend and contemporary Siegfried Kracauer. The result of this reception was that his artwork essay quickly took on a canonical power. To this day, the artwork essay is cited more than any other across the varied disciplines in which he is now read.

Benjamin's reception across these disciplines and within more recent critical approaches also reveals a general characteristic: a relatively small selection of his works tends to be cited (most notably, his analysis of allegory, the work of art essay, "The Author as Producer," "On the Concept of History," and, since its translation, *The Arcades Project*). An equally striking second characteristic has been a tendency to extract those sentences and phrases that lend themselves to citation as authoritative insights. Sustained analysis of the development of his ideas, the arguments he makes in relation to them, and his relation to the work of contemporaries is more frequently absent than present as Benjamin's work spreads across the humanities and social sciences. The manner of this reception has certainly bolstered his status as an interdisciplinary icon; however, it does pose the question of who this Benjamin is when his ideas and concepts are splintered throughout much of the critical activity of the late twentieth century, and not always in the way he understood them. Perhaps the way to pose this question is the way Benjamin addressed the question of his own significance: "Am I the one who is called W. B. or am I simply called W. B.?" As the effect of an expanded range of his writings in English takes hold, the task of addressing fully not just what Benjamin means for us but also what he meant within the intellectual and historical context that marked his writings can begin in earnest. Then the answer to what is received in the name of Benjamin will be less splintered, as the complexity of his writing and his insistence on a continuity in the development of his career comes to the fore.

Notes

1 Life

1 "Curriculum Vitae," *GS* 7.2, 532.
2 *Ibid.*
3 "Instruction and Evaluation," *GS* 2.1, 37.
4 *The Correspondence of Walter Benjamin and Gershom Scholem 1932–1940*, 27.
5 *Ibid.*

2 Contexts

1 Cited by Robert Norton in *Secret Germany: Stefan George and His Circle* (Ithaca, NY: Cornell University Press, 2002), 434.
2 *Ibid.*
3 Bertolt Brecht, *Brecht on Theatre* (New York: Hill and Wang, 1992), 42.

3 Works

1 As Benjamin notes, the Iena Romantics did not distinguish between art and literature although when they used the word art, literature was invariably what they referred to. *The Concept of Criticism in German Romanticism* will be referred to subsequently as *The Concept of Criticism.*
2 "Selbstanzeige der Dissertation," *GS* 1.2, 708.
3 In a work that presents a fundamental distinction between tragedy and the Baroque mourning play, it is somewhat unfortunate that the title *Origin of the German Tragic Drama* has been used in the translation even if they should both share some qualities of the tragic. For Benjamin, they have a very different relation to history and it is on this basis that he distinguishes tragedy and mourning plays from one another. In order to retain Benjamin's distinction, "mourning play" will be used to refer to the *Trauerspiel*.
4 Theodor Adorno, "Benjamin's *Einbahnstrasse*," in *Über Walter Benjamin* (Frankfurt: Suhrkamp, 1968), 53.
5 Karl Kraus, *Die Fackel* 376/377 (May 30, 1913), 21.

146

6 Brecht uses the term literarization in the third of his Notebooks published in 1931. Benjamin would already be familiar with Brecht's thinking on this concept from his conversations with Brecht prior to this date.

7 Johann Jakob Bachofen (1815–87), a Swiss social anthropologist and jurist. Benjamin refers to his 1861 book, *Mother Right.* In late 1934 to early 1935 Benjamin wrote an unpublished essay on Bachofen (see *SW* 3, 11–24).

8 The third version is the form in which this essay is best known and it is the one referred to here.

9 Adorno, "Portrait of Walter Benjamin," in *Prisms* (Cambridge, MA: MIT Press, 1983), 239.

4 Critical reception

1 Jürgen Habermas, "Consciousness-Raising or Redemptive Criticism: The Contemporaneity of Walter Benjamin," *New German Critique* 17 (Spring 1979), 32.

2 Commemorating Walter Benjamin. *Diacritics* 22: 3–4 (Autumn–Winter, 1992), 69–80.

3 Jacques Derrida, "Force of Law," in *Acts of Religion*, ed. Gil Anidjar (New York: Routledge, 2002), 298.

4 Jules David Prown, "In Pursuit of Culture: The Formal Language of Objects," *American Art* 9.2 (1995), 2.

Guide to further reading

Works

German

Gesammelte Schriften. 7 vols. Ed. Rolf Tiedemann and Hermann
    Schweppenhäuser. Frankfurt: Suhrkamp, 1972–89.

English

The Arcades Project. Trans. Howard Eiland and Kevin McLaughlin. Cambridge,
    MA: Harvard University Press, 1999.
Charles Baudelaire: A Lyric Poet in the Era of High Capitalism. Trans. Harry Zohn.
    London: New Left Books, 1973.
Illuminations. Ed. Hannah Arendt. Trans. Harry Zohn. New York: Schocken
    Books, 1969.
Moscow Diary. Trans. Richard Sieburth. Ed. Gary Smith. Cambridge, MA:
    Harvard University Press, 1986.
One-Way Street and Other Writings. Trans. Edward Jephcott and K. Shorter.
    London: New Left Books, 1979.
Origin of the German Tragic Drama. Trans. John Osborne. London: New Left
    Books, 1977.
Reflections: Essays, Aphorisms, Autobiographical Writings. Trans. Edmund
    Jephcott. Ed. Peter Demetz. New York: Schocken, 1986.
Selected Writings 1913–1926. Vol. 1. Ed. Marcus Bullock and Michael W.
    Jennings. Cambridge, MA: Harvard University Press, 1996.
Selected Writings 1927–1934. Vol. 2. Trans. Rodney Livingstone *et al.* Ed. Michael
    W. Jennings, Howard Eiland, and Gary Smith. Cambridge, MA: Harvard
    University Press, 1999.
Selected Writings 1925–1938. Vol. 3. Trans. Edmund Jephcott, Howard Eiland
    et al. Ed. Howard Eiland and Michael W. Jennings. Cambridge, MA:
    Harvard University Press, 2002.
Selected Writings 1938–1940. Vol. 4. Trans. Edmund Jephcott *et al.* Ed. Howard
    Eiland and Michael W. Jennings. Cambridge, MA: Harvard University
    Press, 2003.
Understanding Brecht. Trans. Anna Bostock. London: New Left Books, 1973.

Letters

Adorno and Benjamin: The Complete Correspondence 1928–1940. Ed. Henry
   Lonitz. Trans. Nicholas Walker. Cambridge, MA: Harvard University
   Press, 1999.
The Correspondence of Walter Benjamin 1920–1940. Ed. Gershom Scholem and
   Theodor W. Adorno. Trans. Manfred R. Jacobson and Evelyn M.
   Jacobson. Chicago: University of Chicago Press, 1994.
The Correspondence of Walter Benjamin and Gershom Scholem, 1932–1940. Trans.
   Gary Smith and André Lefevre. New York: Schocken Books, 1989.
Gesammelte Briefe. 6 vols. Ed. Christoph Gödde and Henri Lonitz. Frankfurt:
   Suhrkamp, 1995–2000.

Selected secondary sources

Contexts

Buck-Morss, Susan. *The Origin of Negative Dialectics: Theodor W. Adorno, Walter
   Benjamin, and the Frankfurt Institute.* New York: Free Press, 1977. Exam-
   ines the Frankfurt School and Benjamin's relation to it from the
   perspective of its method of negative dialectics.
Gay, Peter. *Weimar Culture: The Outsider as Insider.* New York: Harper and Row,
   1968. An introduction to the various intellectual, artistic, social, and
   political movements that developed during the Weimar period in
   Germany.
Jay, Martin. *The Dialectical Imagination: A History of the Frankfurt School and the
   Institute for Social Research, 1923–1950.* Berkeley: University of
   California Press, 1996. Good introduction to the history of the
   Frankfurt School and its development.
Laqueur, Walter Z. *Young Germany: A History of the German Youth Movement.*
   New York: Basic Books, 1962. Provides a history of the various youth
   movements that arose in Germany between 1896 and 1933.
Norton, Robert. *Secret Germany: Stefan George and His Circle.* Ithaca, NY: Cornell
   University Press, 2002. Definitive account of Stefan George and a history
   of the figures associated with his circle.

Biography

Brodersen, Momme. *Walter Benjamin: A Biography.* London: Verso, 1996. A
   full-length biography of Benjamin, useful but whets the appetite for a
   more complete biography with better organization.
Eiland, Howard, and Jennings, Michael. *The Author as Producer: A Life of Walter
   Benjamin.* Cambridge, MA: Harvard University Press, 2007. First

full-length critical biography in English. Situates critical introductions to Benjamin's major works within a full account of his life.

Leslie, Esther. *Walter Benjamin.* London: Reaktion Books, 2007. First biography in English to incorporate fully the German editions of Benjamin's collected writings and letters. Links his personal history to a detailed account of his intellectual development and its social context.

Missac, Pierre. *Walter Benjamin's Passages.* Cambridge, MA: MIT Press, 1995. An account of Benjamin's life interwoven with topics and themes from his works told by someone who knew him during his final years in Paris.

Scholem, Gershom. *Walter Benjamin: The Story of a Friendship.* Philadelphia: Jewish Publication Society of America, 1981. Account of Benjamin's life through Scholem's eyes. Tends to emphasize the Jewish and Messianic aspect of Benjamin's writings.

Witte, Bernd. *Walter Benjamin: An Intellectual Biography.* Trans. James Rolleston. Detroit: Wayne State University Press, 1991. An interpretative biography that emphasizes Benjamin's works and ideas as well as his intellectual contexts.

Selected criticism (books only)

Benjamin, Andrew. Ed. *Adorno and Benjamin: Problems of Modernity.* London: Routledge, 1989. Collection of essays on questions relating to the concept of modernity in both Benjamin and Adorno. Essays treat the enlightenment, modernism, the postmodern, language, feminism, Baudelaire, and Jewish motifs.

Ed. *Walter Benjamin's Philosophy: Destruction and Experience.* Manchester: Clinamen Press, 2000. Collection of essays organized around the philosophical significance of Benjamin's work. Essays treat destruction, violence, tradition, experience, politics, language, time, the work of art essay.

Ed. *Walter Benjamin and Art.* London: Continuum, 2005. Collection of essays on the aesthetic (and its relation to politics), aura, music, revolution, the technological, and photography.

Ed. *Walter Benjamin and History.* London: Continuum, 2005. Collection of essays examining the image, photography, time, architecture, modernity, tradition, and the messianic in relation to Benjamin's concept of history.

Buci-Glucksmann, Christine. *Baroque Reason: The Aesthetics of Modernity.* London: Sage Publications, 1994. Examines the significance of a Baroque reason for the problems that arise within the representation of modernity, namely alienation, melancholy, and nostalgia. Discusses Benjamin's analysis of the Baroque in the context of Nietzsche, Adorno, Musil, Barthes, and Lacan.

Buck-Morss, Susan. *The Dialectics of Seeing: Walter Benjamin and the Arcades Project.* Cambridge, MA: MIT Press, 1989. An inventive reconstruction of Benjamin's fragmentary last work, *The Arcades Project.* Published before this work became available in translation.

Cadava, Eduardo. *Words of Light: Theses on the Photography of History.* Princeton: Princeton University Press, 1997. Focuses on Benjamin's thought and writing through the prism offered by the place of photography in his work.

Caygill, Howard. *Walter Benjamin: The Color of Experience.* London: Routledge, 1998. Extensive examination of the concept of experience and especially visual experience in Benjamin's writings.

Cohen, Margaret. *Profane Illumination: Walter Benjamin and the Paris Surrealist Revolution.* Berkeley: University of California Press, 1993. Unsurpassed and comprehensive account of Benjamin and surrealism within the context of Parisian culture and history during the 1930s.

Eagleton, Terry. *Walter Benjamin: or Towards a Revolutionary Criticism.* London: New Left Books, 1981. An attempt to rescue Benjamin for contemporary Marxist criticism.

Fenves, Peter. *Arresting Language: From Leibniz to Benjamin.* Stanford: Stanford University Press, 2001. Examines how Benjamin's writings on language belong to a history in which language is understood as an interruption of continuous processes and procedures.

Ferris, David. Ed. *Walter Benjamin: Theoretical Questions.* Stanford: Stanford University Press, 1993. Collection of essays on theoretical aspects of Benjamin's works. Essays on aura, history, the poetic, presentation, language and the autobiographical, and violence, as well as his reading of Romanticism.

Ed. *The Cambridge Companion to Walter Benjamin.* Cambridge: Cambridge University Press, 2004. Collection of essays examining the avant-garde, art forms, language and mimesis, cultural history, modernity, psychoanalysis, Romanticism, dialectical materialism, the phantasmagorical, and the autobiographical.

Fischer, Gerhard. *"With the Sharpened Axe of Reason": Approaches to Walter Benjamin.* Oxford: Berg, 1996. Collection of essays by Australian and European critics on modernity, gender, criticism and literature, and performance and theatricality in Benjamin's writings.

Gilloch, Graeme. *Myth and Metropolis: Walter Benjamin and the City.* Cambridge: Polity Press, 1996. Focuses on the place of the city within Benjamin's thought. Explores surrealism and modernity as well as Marx and Freud in relation to Benjamin.

Critical Constellations. Cambridge: Polity Press, 2002. Thematic account of Benjamin's writings. Emphasizes the relation between fragmentation and constellation.

Gumbrecht, Hans Ulrich, and Marrinan, Michael. *Mapping Benjamin: The Work of Art in the Digital Age.* Stanford: Stanford University Press, 2003. Collection of short essays that respond to the question of Benjamin's contemporary significance for a range of disciplines in the humanities as well as some of the social sciences.

Hanssen, Beatrice. *Walter Benjamin's Other History: Of Stones, Animals, Human Beings, and Angels*. Berkeley: University of California Press, 1998. Focuses on Benjamin's *Origin of the German Tragic Drama* and examines the complexities of his understanding of history as developed in this work.

Ed. *Walter Benjamin and* The Arcades Project. London: Routledge, 2006. Collection of essays by American and British critics on issues and concepts in Benjamin's uncompleted work on the Paris Arcades.

Hanssen, Beatrice, and Benjamin, Andrew. *Walter Benjamin and Romanticism*. London: Continuum, 2002. Collection of essays by American, British and European critics on different aspects of Romanticism examined by Benjamin in his early formative writings.

Jacobs, Carol. *In the Language of Walter Benjamin*. Baltimore: Johns Hopkins University Press, 1999. Close readings that examine the performance of language in Benjamin's autobiographical writings as well as his essays on language and translation.

Jameson, Fredric. *Marxism and Form: Twentieth Century Dialectical Theories of Literature*. Princeton, NJ: Princeton University Press, 1971. Contains the earliest account in English of Benjamin as a Marxist critic.

Jennings, Michael W. *Dialectical Images: Walter Benjamin's Theory of Literary Criticism*. Ithaca, NY: Cornell University Press, 1987. Places Benjamin's writings on Baudelaire, the philosophy of history, experience, truth in relation to a theory of criticism.

Lane, Richard J. *Walter Benjamin: Writing through the Catastrophe*. Manchester: Manchester University Press, 2005. Examines the relation between philosophy and theology across Benjamin's writings. Analyzes this relation in the German youth movements, the George Circle, and surrealism. Also examines Benjamin's concepts of experience and the work of art as well as his textual practice.

Leslie, Esther. *Walter Benjamin: Overpowering Conformism*. London: Pluto Press, 2000. Offers a more political reading of Benjamin in the wake of the theoretical attention given to his works in the 1980s and 1990s.

McCole, John. *Walter Benjamin and the Antinomies of Tradition*. Ithaca, NY: Cornell University Press, 1993. Examines Benjamin's intellectual development while emphasizing an engagement with tradition that can be traced from his early writings. Treats Romanticism, experience, allegory, surrealism, memory, and history.

Mehlman, Jeffrey. *Walter Benjamin for Children: An Essay on His Radio Years*. Chicago: University of Chicago Press, 1993. An analysis of thirty scripts Benjamin wrote for radio broadcasts between 1929 and 1933 in the context of his larger critical concerns.

Nägele, Rainer. Ed. *Benjamin's Ground*. Detroit: Wayne State University Press, 1988. Close textual readings of major aspects of Benjamin's thought. Essays on language, Baudelaire, lyric, and the image.

Theatre, Theory, Speculation: Walter Benjamin and the Scenes of Modernity. Baltimore: Johns Hopkins University Press, 1991. Extensive analysis of *Origin of the German Tragic Drama* that traces the consequences of Benjamin's account of how modernity is formed within the Baroque.

Pensky, Max. *Melancholy Dialectics.* Amherst: University of Massachusetts Press, 1993. Extensive analysis of melancholy as a central force within Benjamin's writings. Treats modernity, allegory, criticism, and history in his thought.

Richter, Gerhard. *Walter Benjamin and the Corpus of Autobiography.* Detroit: Wayne State University Press, 2000. Examines Benjamin's autobiographical writings and their emphasis on the body and its image as a crucial site for his engagement with political questions and concerns.

Ed. *Benjamin's Ghosts: Interventions in Contemporary Literary and Cultural Theory.* Stanford: Stanford University Press, 2002. Collection of essays that examines Benjamin's contemporary critical significance. Essays by German and American critics on cinema, image, aura, art, history, language, the tragic, *The Arcades Project*, and Benjamin's concept of the constellation.

Roberts, Julian. *Walter Benjamin.* Atlantic Highlands, NJ: Humanities Press, 1983. Short general account of Benjamin's writings.

Rochlitz, Rainer. *The Disenchantment of Art: The Philosophy of Walter Benjamin.* Trans. Jane Marie Todd. New York: Guilford, 1996. Systematic treatment of Benjamin's thought emphasizing his philosophy of language, aesthetic concerns, and historical thought.

Smith, Gary, Ed. *On Walter Benjamin: Critical Essays and Recollections.* Cambridge, MA: MIT Press, 1988. Wide range of essays on Benjamin as well as personal recollections. Includes some important essays first published in Germany in the 1970s and early 1980s.

Ed. *Benjamin: Philosophy, Aesthetics, History.* Chicago: University of Chicago Press, 1989. Essays by American and German authors on Benjamin. Essays focus on the concept of progress, the work of art essay, history, materialism, the messianic, and *The Arcades Project*.

Steinberg, Michael P. Ed. *Walter Benjamin and the Demands of History.* Ithaca, NY: Cornell University Press, 1996. Essays on Benjamin's understanding of history, both cultural and philosophical, as well as applications of his historical thought to modern cultural contexts.

Weber, Samuel. *Mass Mediauras: Form, Technics, Media.* Stanford: Stanford University Press, 2001. Locates Benjamin's writings within a transformation of artistic form and experience that marks the transition from a work-based to a media-based model in art and culture.

Benjamin's -abilities. Cambridge, MA: Harvard University Press, 2008. Innovative study of a series of key concepts that all share the same suffix in Benjamin's writings. Concepts discussed include impartibility, criticizability, citability, translatability, and reproducibility.

Weigel, Sigrid. *Body- and Image-Space: Re-Reading Walter Benjamin.* London: Routledge, 1996. Examines the relation of image and body as a central issue within Benjamin's work. Treats gender, allegory, and the dialectical image, as well as the relation of Foucault and Kristeva to Benjamin's writings.

Wolin, Richard. *Walter Benjamin: An Aesthetic of Redemption.* Revised edition. Berkeley: University of California Press, 1994. A broad account of some of the principal questions, issues, and concepts framing Benjamin's critical development.

Index

Adorno, Theodor Wiesengrund 11, 14,
    17, 18, 27–28, 112, 115, 118,
    122, 125–26, 130, 136, 138
aesthetics 33, 47, 49–50, 60, 86–87, 91,
    99–101, 104, 106–07, 126, 140
Anfang, Der (journal) 3, 5, 23
Arendt, Hannah 137, 138
Atget, Eugène 95
avant-garde 25

Bakunin, Mikhail 79
Baudelaire, Charles 7, 114, 116, 123,
    128–31
    Les Fleurs du mal 62
    "To a Woman Passing by" 126
Baroque 10, 125, 130, 142
    drama 11, 47, 67, 71, 72
Bataille, Georges 19
Benjamin, Walter
    Topics and concepts
    absolute 32, 34, 45, 49, 60
    allegory 71–73, 142; and ruin
        72–73, 142
    appearance 50, 57, 59–61, 94
    artistic production 30, 99
    aura 18, 94, 105, 108, 112, 113,
        125, 138
    bohème 123, 125
    commodity fetish 117–18, 121,
        126, 127
    constellation 69–70, 72, 119, 120,
        131
    convolutes 115, 120
    creative spirit 30, 32

criticism/critique 10, 14, 29, 32,
    46, 52, 56, 58, 59
criticism of: academia 11;
    capitalist industry 92; culture
    11, 77, 136, 143; history 32, 48,
    119, 120; interpretation 9, 141,
    142; journalism 88–90;
    literature 139; materialism 90;
    modernity 49, 142; politics 14,
    86, 101, 115, 121; reputation
    12; theory 8, 28, 109, 138
Denkbilder (thought images) 74,
    77
dialectical image 118, 120–21
dialectical materialism 91
dialectical thought 18
distraction (*Zerstreuung*) 109–10
Eros 31
experience 42–45, 76, 77, 79, 83,
    86, 94, 104, 107–08, 111–13,
    126–30 *Erfahrung* 111, 113,
    127, 129; *Erlebnis* 128
expressionless 58, 60–61, 90
fantastic 117
fashion 117
Flâneur 115, 123, 125–27
historical-problematic 48, 130
history 32, 71, 76, 113, 116, 117,
    120, 127, 132, 134 art 72, 94,
    105, 130; and ruin 71
idea 37, 43, 48, 69–72, 78 of art
    48–49
ideal 35, 58–59
immanent criticism 30, 35

155

The Cambridge Introductions to . . .

AUTHORS

Jane Austen Janet Todd

Samuel Beckett Ronan McDonald

Walter Benjamin David Ferris

Joseph Conrad John Peters

Jacques Derrida Leslie Hill

Emily Dickinson Wendy Martin

George Eliot Nancy Henry

T. S. Eliot John Xiros Cooper

William Faulkner Theresa M. Towner

F. Scott Fitzgerald Kirk Curnutt

Michel Foucault Lisa Downing

Robert Frost Robert Faggen

Nathaniel Hawthorne Leland S. Person

Zora Neale Hurston Lovalerie King

James Joyce Eric Bulson

Herman Melville Kevin J. Hayes

Sylvia Plath Jo Gill

Edgar Allan Poe Benjamin F. Fisher

Ezra Pound Ira Nadel

Shakespeare Emma Smith

Harriet Beecher Stowe Sarah Robbins

Mark Twain Peter Messent

Walt Whitman M. Jimmie Killingsworth

Virginia Woolf Jane Goldman

W. B. Yeats David Holdeman

TOPICS

The American Short Story Martin Scofield

Creative Writing David Morley

Early English Theatre Janette Dillon

English Theatre, 1660–1900 Peter Thomson

Francophone Literature Patrick Corcoran

Modernism Pericles Lewis

Modern Irish Poetry Justin Quinn

Narrative (second edition) H. Porter Abbott

The Nineteenth-Century American Novel Gregg Crane

Postcolonial Literatures C. L. Innes

Russian Literature Caryl Emerson

Shakespeare's Comedies Penny Gay

Shakespeare's History Plays Warren Chernaik

Shakespeare's Tragedies Janette Dillon

The Short Story in English Adrian Hunter

Theatre Studies Christopher Balme

Tragedy Jennifer Wallace